GW01044790

SPEED

Tom McNab

Illustrations by David Gifford

SACKVILLE BOOKS

First published in 1989
by Sackville Books Ltd,
Stradbroke, Suffolk, England
© Sackville Books Limited 1989
© Text Tom McNab

Designed and produced by Sackville Design Group Ltd
Art Editor: Rolando Ugolini
Editor: Nick Bevan

British Library Cataloguing in Publication Data
McNab, Tom, 1933 —
   Speed — (Sackville Sports Clinic)
   1. Athletics. Running — Bibliographies
   I. Time
   796.4'26

ISBN 0 948615 23 0

Typeset by BPCC Printec Ltd, Diss, Norfolk, England.

Reproduction by BPCC Zambril Ltd, Bury St Edmunds, Suffolk,
England.

Printed and bound in Belgium by
Proost Internationale Boekproduktie NV, Turnhout.

Contents

	Introduction	4
1	Born to speed	5
2	Anatomy of speed	8
3	Warm up	16
4	Sprinting	18
5	The start	23
6	Relays	30
7	Isolation drills	36
8	Middle-distance running	46
9	Hurdles	52
10	Long jump	62
11	Triple jump	67
12	Weight-training	70
13	Circuit training	74
14	Plyometrics	76
15	Mobility	78
	Index	80

Introduction

Speed has always fascinated man and the greatest honours have always gone to the athletes who have learned to express themselves in speed of movement.

Speed in its pure form is most simply demonstrated in sprinting. It is important in all races up to 10,000 metres, but clearly becomes less crucial the longer the distance.

In technical events (long jump, triple jump, hurdles) it is just one element, of varying importance, amongst others such as flight-technique and jumping power. So, for the purposes of this book, we are looking at speed in various specific contexts.

Maybe you already run at club level or perhaps you are about to join a club or are a coach. Whatever your interest, you will need a plan of campaign — a manual to follow.

Speed is a skill you can learn — by training, by drills — and, although it is always easiest to learn when you have a good model on which to base your technique, I believe that it is as simple, satisfying and enjoyable to learn if you follow good instructions and know what to 'feel' for when you run. The 'feel' can create reference points to which you can constantly return.

Tom McNab

CHAPTER ONE

Born to Speed

Sprinting speed is probably the most natural of all athletic attributes — the most inborn and difficult to manufacture without inherent ability. Many of the great sprinters (1936 Olympic 100 and 200 metres gold medallist Jesse Owens is a good example) have been capable of running 100 metres in around 10.50 seconds with little training as early as their late teens. Subsequent training whittled Owens' time down to 10.30 seconds, a mere 2% improvement. A talented middle-distance runner in his mid teens, might run 1500 metres in 4 minutes 40 seconds before training. Six years later, after training, he may have reduced the time for the same distance to 3 minutes 45 seconds, an improvement of almost 20%!

   These dramatic improvements occur because training can substantially improve the efficiency of the heart, lungs and muscle capillary system — the factors on which middle-distance runners depend. Speed is less susceptible to training — but that's not to say that it can't be substantially improved. I have worked with athletes who have achieved massive improvements in the 10-12% area (perhaps reducing a time for 100 metres from 12.2 to 11.1 seconds) between the ages of 17 and 24. This sort of improvement lifted 17 year old Andrea Lynch from a club-level athlete in1969 to world class by 1973. Daley Thompson, a naturally fast runner, who logged the equivalent of 100 metres in 10.90 seconds (electrical timing) at the age of 16, has also achieved a 6% improvement, cutting his time to 10.26 seconds at his peak, without the benefit of specialist sprint training.

Pure speed

What is 'pure speed' in sprinting? It's different from the ability to move from inertia — the 0-40 metre phase of sprinting (this is acceleration). It's also different in the mixture of leverage, power and technique used. So, some athletes are only average in acceleration, but outstanding in mid race and the final 40 metres. Only an athlete with exceptional 'pure speed' can sustain the lead given by a good start — and as Ben Johnson has proved, this is a technique which can be learned through training.

   Sprinting speed relates to explosive power and muscle-speed and has more bearing on middle- and long-distance running. Indeed, the only real use the sprinter has for stamina is for keeping up levels of training and being able to undertake a good volume of practice.

Built for speed

Training is essential — but physical make-up, muscular build and metabolism play a vital role. A natural sprinter's muscles are quite different from those of an endurance-runner (see Anatomy of Speed). They work in short, immensely powerful bursts, as opposed to the prolonged, less vigorous action of a middle-distance athlete. You have to accept that great sprinters are, in essence, born and not made.

Speed training for women

In most physical sports, different levels of exertion and capacity — and therefore achievement — are expected of men and women — however, when it comes to training for speed, women are just as capable of undertaking rigorous training as men.

Unlike long-distance events where time differentials between men and women are substantial, the differences between men's and women's 100-metre bests are very small. When men can just break the 10-second barrier and women are now running the distance in around 10.50 seconds, the levels of training to achieve these times are likely to be very similar whoever the runner.

Charisma of speed

You have only to see the pure elation on Florence Griffith-Joyner's face as she powered to record-breaking victory in the 100 and 200 metres Olympic finals in Seoul, to understand the sheer exhilaration of a body running in perfect balance — no movements wasted — at a speed no other woman has ever achieved.

At world-class level sprinting is a very high-profile sport — after all, it's a world-shaking achievement to be recognised as the fastest man or woman on earth. Sprinting has tremendous charisma too — identifying with national and local heroes such as Linford Christie and his 1988 Olympic 100 metre silver medal has undoubtedly given hundreds of aspiring athletes the encouragement they needed to take up the sport seriously.

The feel of speed

Speed, whether it's over 100 metres or 1500 metres, is enhanced by the runner's mental approach and their desire to succeed. You need motivation and determination to keep training, practising and persevering to whittle 10ths of a second off your personal best. Sometimes what is missing to attain a best-ever performance is the 'feel', whether it is flowing, pushing, stretching or finding the ideal balance. Emulating the classic style of a particular world-class athlete and visualising yourself looking like them as you run can improve performance immensely. What the world-class athletes have is exactly the right feel as they run — so don't just train, go for the feeling as described in this book.

Sporting speed

When you train for speed, you increase your explosive muscle power and in doing so you'll find you're better equipped for other sports which call for running ability — rugby, hockey, soccer, squash and tennis. Training for speed will not do anything for your eye/hand co ordination, but a speedy, well-tuned body is bound to play a better game.

Training intensity

An international-class athlete must train every day, but for club runners with jobs, studies and other demands on their time, training sessions are necessarily fewer.

The number of sessions you take in a week of actual running practice, specific sport training, isolation drills and weights/mobility/circuits/plyometrics work-outs depends on your degree of fitness, your aspirations and dedication.

Whatever the intensity of your training — and it has to be said that irregular sessions without clear progression will never achieve any improvements — you must find a balance between the different types of training.

If, for instance, you are training for pure sprinting speed, you may fit in three sessions of sprint training with isolation drills and two in a gym with weights etc. If you aim for middle-distance speed, you need to concentrate on actual running over distances to promote speed-endurance, and if your use of speed is in some other branch of the sport such as the long jump, then specific speed drills are needed.

Only by performing high-quality work can you learn good running habits. Most of all, remember to enjoy yourself!

CHAPTER TWO

Anatomy of speed

If you understand how your muscles work and get their
energy and what happens to them in fatigue, it will be clearer
why some bodies lend themselves to sprinting speed, others
to endurance — and others to no sort of running at all! Also,
you can see why training is able to bring about improvements
in your performance.

To start with, let's look at muscles. To move at all, your
muscles have to be prompted by a current or electrical current
from the brain.

The sort of fast, powerful contraction by the large muscles
of the legs, which is essential for sprinting requires a strong
electrical current — perhaps as many as 70 impulses per
second for full-speed running, while smaller, less powerful
movements need a current of as few as five impulses a
second. This just goes to show the enormous range of power
levels at which your body can operate, responding to the
demands you place on it.

Large-diameter nerves carry the strong electrical impulses
which produce bursts of powerful movement — the wider the
diameter the nerves, the greater force of current they can
carry. It follows that natural sprinters' muscles are driven
mainly by strong impulses, and endurance-runners' muscles
are powered by weaker impulses which arrive by smaller-
diameter nerves.

Although you will have an inherent tendency towards one
of these muscle types or the other, it doesn't mean to say
that you cannot improve on your speed if you are an
endurance runner, or increase your stamina if you sprint —
it's just the basic aptitude which you are born with which you
cannot change.

Muscle make-up

Muscles are made up of tens of thousands of individual fibres,
held together by connective tissue which weaves in and
around them, running parallel to them and encasing the whole
muscle. This connective tissue changes at both ends of the
muscle into tendon, which binds the muscle to the skeleton
and enables muscle-force to be transmitted directly to bones.

What differentiates the sprinter from the distance-runner is
the type of fibre of which their muscles are mainly composed.

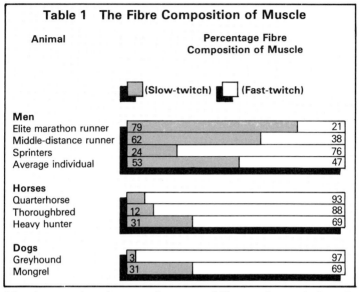

Table 1   The Fibre Composition of Muscle

Animal	Percentage Fibre Composition of Muscle	
	▪ (Slow-twitch)	▫ (Fast-twitch)
Men		
Elite marathon runner	79	21
Middle-distance runner	62	38
Sprinters	24	76
Average individual	53	47
Horses		
Quarterhorse		93
Thoroughbred	12	88
Heavy hunter	31	69
Dogs		
Greyhound	3	97
Mongrel	31	69

Muscles consist of two main types of fibre — fast-twitch and slow-twitch. The fast-twitch fibres can produce large forces quickly, but only for short periods of time. The slow-twitch fibres produce lower levels of power but, because of their superior ability to pick up oxygen, can work for much longer periods.

Marathon-runners' muscles have almost 80% slow-twitch fibre, while sprinters' have almost the same amount of fast-twitch. A middle-distance runner has 62/38 slow/fast-twitch fibres because of the combination of speed and endurance which such an event demands. No marathon-runner could stay close to a sprinter in an 800-metre race. This would produce vast amounts of muscle-waste which the most marvellous heart-lung system would be unable to disperse quickly enough — by 400 metres he would be reduced to a trot. Conversely, if the distance were a marathon, involving a speed of about 5 minutes per mile, and a middle-distance runner tried to stay the course with a seasoned marathon man, he would eventually have to engage fast-twitch fibres which would have difficulty in meeting his long-term needs and I suspect the marathon-runner would probably leave him just beyond half way and win by a margin of about 15 minutes. On the other hand, a classic sprinter such as Carl Lewis with 80% fast-twitch fibre would 'die' in an international 800-metre race and would probably be unable to complete a marathon.

9

Table 2 Oxygen to energy

The VO$_2$ maximum levels which different events demand.
The figures refer to the mililitres of oxygen per minute which the body can process into energy, per kg of body weight.

	Men ((ml/kg)/min)	Women ((ml/kg)/min)
Endurance sports		
Long-distance running	75-80	65-70
Cross-country skiing	75-78	65-70
Biathlon	75-78	-
Road cycling	70-75	60-65
Middle-distance running	70-75	65-68
Skating	65-72	55-60
Orienteering	65-72	60-65
Swimming	60-70	55-60
Rowing	65-69	60-64
Track racing	65-70	55-60
Canoeing	60-68	50-55
Walking	60-65	55-60
Power sports		
Sprint (200m track)	55-60	45-50
Sprint track and field (100m, 200m)	48-52	43-47
Long jump	50-55	45-50
Competition consisting of several events (decathlon, septathlon)	60-65	50-55
Nordic combination (15km ski walking and ski jumping)	60-65	-
Weight lifting	40-50	-
Discus throwing, shot putting	40-45	35-40
Javelin throwing	45-50	42-47
Pole vaulting	45-50	-
Ski jumping	40-45	-

Within a single body, muscle make-up is complex. Biopsies have revealed that different types of sportsmen have differing balances of fast and slow-twitch fibres in specific muscles, depending on their use. A cross-country skier, for example, may have 90% fast-twitch fibre in his triceps which he uses to propel himself on his poles, but 95% slow-twitch endurance fibre in his hamstrings because of their work in kicking and gliding. In contrast, a sprinter will invariably have around 90% fast-twitch fibres in his quadriceps and only 50-60% fast-twitch fibre in his arm and shoulder muscles.

The classic sprinters in the animal world are the quarter-horse and the greyhound, which have around 97/3 fast/slow-twitch muscle composition. The American quarter-horse is so called because it is raced over a straight quarter of a mile, where it can generate speeds approaching 45 mph. It has no staying power beyond this distance. Similarly, the greyhound's maximum range is about 450 metres, though its speed is a little lower than that of the quarter-horse, essentially because it runs on a tightly curved track.

This oversimplifies the situation, since man has a third intermediate type of fibre which can, stimulated by training, go either way, and this may explain the ability of some runners to move successfully up or down a distance. But, for practical purposes, we are locked into our genetic inheritance and there is no way by which a carthorse can be made into a race-horse. But it is possible to produce a faster carthorse.

Muscle power

Just as there are two basic types of muscle fibre, there are two different types of fitness — aerobic and anaerobic. Aerobic fitness literally means 'with air', and anaerobic means 'without air' — or more specifically, oxygen. Aerobic exercise uses oxygen to release energy, and requires not only well trained muscles, but an efficient cardio-respiratory system (heart and lungs) to deliver oxygen to them.

The heart, lungs and blood vessels work to deliver oxygen and carry away CO_2 and other waste — it is up to the muscles to process the oxygen into energy. The aim of aerobic endurance training is to raise the heart rate to a level to cope with the performance required, and then sustain it there. Anaerobic fitness is the ability to produce sharp bursts of high energy — not using oxygen but from chemicals which are present in the muscles. This type of fitness therefore does not depend on the heart/lung system. From this it emerges that for fast sprinting over short distances, the fitness required is mainly anaerobic, and for endurance running, it is of an aerobic variety.

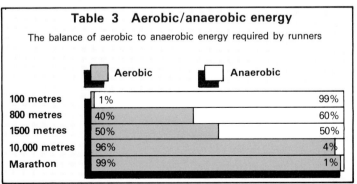

Table 3 Aerobic/anaerobic energy

The balance of aerobic to anaerobic energy required by runners

	Aerobic	Anaerobic
100 metres	1%	99%
800 metres	40%	60%
1500 metres	50%	50%
10,000 metres	96%	4%
Marathon	99%	1%

The male muscular and skeletal system

Muscles are designed to make the body move. They are grouped in well organized systems for greater efficiency. The essence of speed is to develop and sustain a well balanced muscle system into which is built the power the body needs. This illustration shows the range and organization of the voluntary muscles. The skeleton is covered with approximately 600 muscles which form about 40 per cent of the body's weight.

 1 Frontalis
 2 Trapezius
 3 Deltoid
 4 Pectoralis major
 5 Triceps brachii
 6 Latissimus dorsi
 7 Biceps brachii
 8 Brachioradialis
 9 Rectus abdominis
10 Pectineus
11 Rectus femoris
12 Vastus lateralis
13 Peroneus longus
14 Peroneus brevis
15 Tibialis anterior
16 Extensor digitorum longus
17 Sphenoid
18 Mandible
19 Hyoid bone
20 Cervical column
21 1st rib
22 Clavicle
23 Scapula
24 Sternum
25 Humerus
26 Costal cartilage
27 12th rib
28 Ulna
29 Sacrum
30 Radius
31 Pelvic inlet
32 Ischium
33 Pubis
34 Carpals
35 Metacarpals

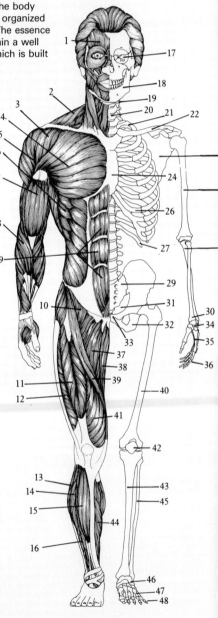

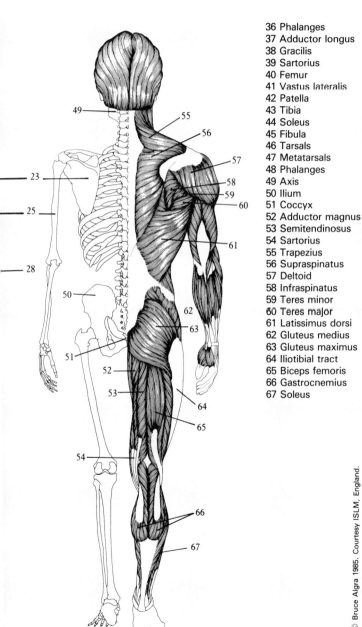

36 Phalanges
37 Adductor longus
38 Gracilis
39 Sartorius
40 Femur
41 Vastus lateralis
42 Patella
43 Tibia
44 Soleus
45 Fibula
46 Tarsals
47 Metatarsals
48 Phalanges
49 Axis
50 Ilium
51 Coccyx
52 Adductor magnus
53 Semitendinosus
54 Sartorius
55 Trapezius
56 Supraspinatus
57 Deltoid
58 Infraspinatus
59 Teres minor
60 Teres major
61 Latissimus dorsi
62 Gluteus medius
63 Gluteus maximus
64 Iliotibial tract
65 Biceps femoris
66 Gastrocnemius
67 Soleus

Training theory shows that there is little point in a sprinter achieving a high level of aerobic fitness — but he needs to have a certain degree in order to undertake adequate volumes of high-quality training, and to recover from such sessions.

This degree of aerobic fitness is measured in a VO_2 level — the capacity of the body to process oxygen into energy. For a sprinter 50-60 ml per kg of body weight per minute is probably an adequate VO_2 level, while for a 400-metre runner, 60-70 would be more suitable. This contrasts with VO_2 levels of 70-80 for a middle-distance runner and 75-85 for the best of long-distance skiers and runners.

Studies have been made on marathon-runners to find out the relationship between their aerobic capacity and their purely anaerobic energy. The tests showed that, in their 100-mile-a-week training period, their vertical jumps were in the region of 30-40 cm. When they cut their mileage by half there was a 50% improvement in their vertical jumps. This is simply because long, slow running, though it improves the condition of the heart and local muscular endurance, reduces the fast-twitch springiness in the leg muscles and the Achilles tendon.

This just goes to show that all technical sprint training needs to be done at the 80% effort level and above — otherwise what you are learning is simply a different kind of running. In effect, you just become a fine slow runner! You only learn to run fast by doing fast things — preferably with fast people — and the best way to improve the strength of your sprint-fibre muscles is by progressive training.

Fatigue

A main cause of muscle fatigue in long-distance running is lack of fuel from which the muscles can produce energy. When muscles run out of glycogen, their main fuel for energy, they start to process fat — but this takes up more oxygen than glycogen to process — so an athlete would need an even stronger cardio-respiratory system to keep the oxygen arriving in sufficient quantities. When this supply fails, fatigue sets in.

It is worth noting that endurance fatigue and sprint fatigue are caused by different mechanisms. In endurance running, fatigue sets in when the muscles become depleted of glycogen and can no longer meet the runner's demands — or they will be damaged. In sprinting, the fatigued muscles still have reserves of glycogen — but the process of producing powerful sprinting energy creates a waste product — lactic acid. This residue raises the acidity of the muscles' environment and eventually blocks its ability to contract.

Fat

Whatever your level of muscular fitness, power/weight ratio is a factor which (quite literally) bulks large! Lean body mass is critical to both speed and endurance as, clearly, fat has no propulsive power — it just gives you more dead weight to transport. In a comprehensive testing of the different build-types which go to make up a rugby team, it was found that the backs (classic sprinter types) had 7-13% body fat; among the forwards these percentages rose to 15-25% and in the props to as high as 20-25%. Certainly anyone looking to improve speed, whether it is for a game or in sprinting itself, must look to their body-fat percentage.

It's important to note that there are male/female differences. Women have, on average, 4-5% more body fat than men — so a top female sprinter would expect to have body fat in the region of 12-16%.

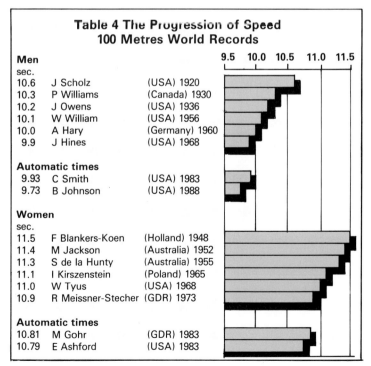

Table 4 The Progression of Speed
100 Metres World Records

CHAPTER THREE

Warm up

Even the local lads playing football on a Sunday morning do a few perfunctory knee-bends and a bit of jogging on the spot before taking to the pitch. They are not just amateur sportsmen posing as professionals, they are carrying out an instinctive ritual to prepare both mind and muscles to go into action.

If you are a competitive athlete, your mental warm-up may start days before an event — but once you have focussed your mind on your objective, you owe it to yourself to ensure that your training doesn't go to waste. You need to bring your body up to readiness for a race — and this goes for every-day training too.

At rest, a muscle's temperature is 37°C. With warm-up it will rise to 43°C, bringing the power of the muscle up by as much as 50% — so temperature is critical in the production of speed. The muscle becomes more relaxed, less likely to tear and, as muscles work in opposing pairs — one contracting, the other relaxing — this rise in temperature means they are capable of greater overall movement and elasticity. All this points to the need for an adequate warm-up before you start.

Why warm up?

A good warm-up has four main functions:

● It raises muscle temperature in order to increase efficiency of movement.
● It minimizes the risk of injury.
● It prepares you psychologically for both competition and training.
● It provides neuro-muscular preparation — that is, it tunes up the skill aspect of your performance.

Since you must carry out your warm-up every time you start a training session or take part in an event, it is as well to make it a standard ritual, one exercise flowing on from another.
Note: Where possible, perform these preliminary exercises in a warm environment or at least wearing a track suit — it will help to minimize the risk of torn muscles.

The best sequence is as follows, gradually increasing the demands you put on your muscles.

1 Jog for up to ten minutes, preferably on grass.
2 Slow-stretching exercises, as for hurdle/sprint mobility
(see page 78).
3 Low-intensity isolation drills (see page 36-45).
4 Striding.

Fig 1. Typical example of slow-stretch exercise

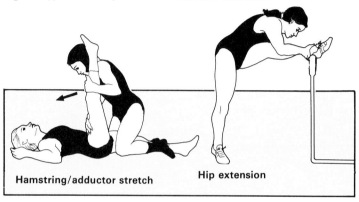

Hamstring/adductor stretch   Hip extension

Fig 2. Typical example of low-intensity isolation drill

Lower leg drill

Competitive and training warm-ups are basically the same,
the essential difference is only the volume of work achieved.
For instance, before training, you may choose to increase the
number and duration of the mobilizing and stretching
exercises because of the conditioning benefits they give.
When you're about to compete, you should have reached the
condition you aimed for — so your objective must be to
limber up your muscles and prepare without draining your
energy for the event.

CHAPTER FOUR

Sprinting

Behind all speed there is necessarily an element of endurance. This is of two types, aerobic and anaerobic, which are achieved by different types of training.

Aerobic and anaerobic endurance training

For aerobic endurance you need a mix of sustained low-level running, interval training and fartlek training (another type of interval exercising). The value of achieving this type of endurance does not relate to actual racing, which does not call upon these energy systems, but rather provides a base for later high-quality work.

Unless a sprinter has a naturally high level of endurance, it is very difficult to achieve the volume of high-quality work necessary to be racing fit. What is needed is a background of aerobic endurance, and the most suitable training methods are interval and fartlek training.

The sprinter also needs anaerobic endurance. This relates to the capacity of the muscles to continue to work at high speed in a state of fatigue, so it relates mostly to the 400-metre distance and to a lesser degree to 100 and 200 metres. This is speed-endurance, a vital component of sprint speed.

Sprint speed

A sprint consists of three elements which appear, to a greater or lesser degree, according to the distance — 100, 200 or 400 metres. With all these, the speed training requirement is the same, with a varying degree of speed-endurance which increases with the distance.

1 Starting speed This relates to the distance from the start to the attainment of top speed, usually about 50 metres for men and 40 metres for women, and it subdivides into speed of reaction and pick-up.

2 Pure speed This running or 'pure' speed is expressed most clearly in the 40-70 metres 'holding' period.

3 Speed-endurance This relates to the decline in speed in the finishing 70-100 metre period, but is more evident in the final 100 metres of a 200-metre race.

Over 200 metres starting speed is less critical and pure speed
(running speed) and speed-endurance (finishing speed) are
more important than over 100 metres. A practical example of
this is Ben Johnson, who has immense power in the 0-60
metre phase, but has never featured as a great 200 metre
runner, probably due to lack of speed-endurance.

In good sprinting, each one of the three elements flows into
the other, although they need to be practised separately and
require different forms of conditioning. They are bound
together in good running technique, which is best expressed
as 'relaxed power'. Good running technique means that all
forward movement is efficiently expressed and involves the
minimum of tense or ineffective action.

Starting speed

You are moving your body from inertia — the first area is
reaction time, the split seconds it takes to get off the blocks.
To show how important this is, in one typical race, Ben
Johnson's reaction time was around 0.126 seconds. In the
same race, Carl Lewis took 0.176 seconds. The difference is
0.050 seconds, and the gap between the two men at the end
of the race is just 0.10 seconds. Half of the final gap between
them lies in reaction time alone.

Can reaction time be improved? All available studies show
that it can. The following reaction practices can help achieve
a faster start and shave time off your race.

1 Starting to the gun, using varying gaps between 'set' and
the report of the gun.
2 Work without the gun, using a hand-clap as the stimulus.
3 Work on the feeling of the gun *releasing* the sprinter, as
opposed to the sprinter reacting to the gun. A good way to
approach this is to imagine you are a vast torrent of water,
held back by the walls of a dam. Suddenly there is a hole in
the dam — you are the water, released, and you rush through
the hole.

Mental pictures

Think of the best starter you know — and watch them until
you can imitate each aspect of their stance and balance.
Visualize them for yourself as you settle on to the blocks, and
imitate them as closely as you can — until you feel that you
must look like them. If you emulate their style, your 'feel' for
starting and for a good push off on release should improve
noticeably.

Acceleration practices

These exercises work to improve pushing power away from the start.

1 Harness running, with the partner exerting varying pressure. You must achieve a full range of movement (see figure 4).

2 Uphill running (see figure 3). Here isolation drills can be used, such as elbow drive (page 39), knee pick-up (page 42) and full leg-extension (page 43). Try isolating one of these aspects on each practice.

Fig 3. Uphill running

Fig 4. Harness running

Leg power

Leg power is vital to starting. You can improve this through weight training (page 70) in the following ways. (You need to repeat these exercises in the area of 6-10 times during the November to January period, reducing to 1-6 times in January to April, then returning to the 6-10 repetition area during the competitive season. Perform four sets of each of these basic exercises.

1 Power clean (page 71)
2 Squat exercise (page 71)
3 High pull (see page 71)

Do all of these exercises explosively, through a full range, working at high speed, making sure you use the correct technique every time.

Arm power

The arms, though less important than the legs, also need to work, in order to balance the thrust of the legs. You should perform these exercises in the 1-10 repetition range.

1 Bench press (page 70)
2 Olympic press
3 Strict curl (page 72)
4 High pull (page 71)

Don't neglect the abdominal and back muscles — they too must be worked because they are the central postural core round which the legs must work.

1 Sit-ups
2 Chinnies (see page 75)
3 Knee tucks (see page 76)

At least one of these exercises must be part of every session in four sets of 20-30 repetitions.

Mobility

Range of movement is essential so that you can exert large forces over a long range off the blocks and throughout the acceleration period. This is particularly important in the hips, knees and ankles. Use the series of flexibility exercises on page 78. On each exercise in a stretching session, hold the position for 20-30 seconds — during a race warm-up, hold for 8-10 seconds.

Plyometrics

These are bounding exercises which improve the explosive power of the legs (see page 76). You can leave these out in the October to November conditioning period, but they should enter the programme in December and build in volume in April to May. Thereafter, drop the volume to 1-2 light sessions per week, as preservation work, so to speak. As in weight training, it is essential that the exercises are performed explosively, with the correct technique. Distance bounding should be in the 20-40 metre range. Again, just as for weights, you should apply the overload principle, increasing the volume of the exercises throughout the training period.

Pure speed training

The isolation drills on page 36 are essential to the pure speed and speed-endurance sections of all sprints, and undoubtedly become more important as the competitive distance rises. Certainly, any loss of running form is more severely punished in the 400 metres than it is in the shorter distances. The following training programmes relate to these two elements in particular.

Pure speed schedules

1 3 sets of 6 × 60 metres at 90-100% effort. Take a 5-minute rest between sets.
2 3 sets of 3 × 100 metres acceleration runs.
3 3 sets of 3 × 100 metres 'hollow sprints' with 30 metres flat out, 30 metres cruise, then 40 metres flat out.

Speed-endurance schedules

1 3 × 300 metres at 90-100% effort. Full rest between runs.
2 3 × 6 × 150 metres at 100% effort.
Full rest between runs.
3 Hollow runs over 300 metres — that is, 100 metres at 100% effort, 100 metres at 80% and 100 metres at 100%.
4 Four acceleration runs over 200 metres.
Full rest between runs.

5 minute rest between sets. You must always maintain good form. When this goes, then it is time to give up the session, as practice does not make perfect — it makes permanent.

CHAPTER FIVE

The start

It may seem heresy to say that Ben Johnson is not, in the technical sense, a particularly good starter. But when you bear in mind that half a metre of his gain over the first 40 metres lies in his reaction time, you can see that only a small part of his first section of the race is gained from block velocity or power over the ground during his pick-up. If you watch him from the front, you see that his first two strides are sideways, indicating a lack of balance. Any improvement in this area, no matter how small, could take him even further away from his rivals in his pick-up period.

All this may seem like technical nit-picking, but since 2/100 second can make the difference between gold and silver 200 metre medal positions, you cannot afford to ignore it.

There are three points to look for in the sprint start:

● A fast reaction to the gun. Table 5 shows the range of reaction times in international athletics.
● A strong, rangy push-out from the blocks, in balance.
● A powerful pick-up through the first 30-40 metres, which takes the sprinter to peak speed, relaxed, in balance and in control

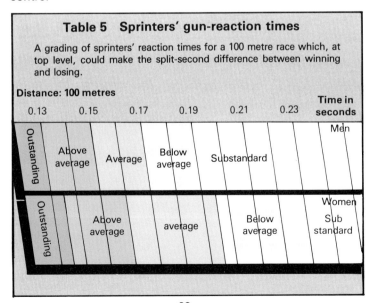

Table 5 Sprinters' gun-reaction times

A grading of sprinters' reaction times for a 100 metre race which, at top level, could make the split-second difference between winning and losing.

Distance: **100 metres**

| 0.13 | 0.15 | 0.17 | 0.19 | 0.21 | 0.23 | Time in seconds |

Men

| Outstanding | Above average | Average | Below average | Substandard |

Women

| Outstanding | Above average | average | Below average | Sub standard |

Starting technique — position

Essential to starting is a position in which the centre of gravity (situated about the navel) is above or slightly beyond the front foot (see figure 5). This means that on the first movement (the release of the hands) the body is immediately moving forwards and that the explosive drive of the front leg can be applied immediately and effectively.

Getting the best front-foot position is a matter of trial and error. A long-legged sprinter of 1.85 metres in height needs a different front-foot position from a short-legged sprinter of the same height. A good rule of thumb for finding the front-foot position is to use one foot length plus the side of the foot. This will give you a working position from which you can make adjustments later.

Another method is simply to place the back knee opposite the instep of the front foot and to move forward with the hands until body-weight is directly over the hands (figure 6).

Which should be the front foot? Quite simply, the strongest leg — the one from which you would make a long jump, as it is the front leg which does most of the work in driving off the blocks when you start.

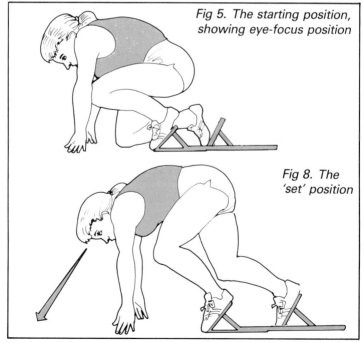

Fig 5. The starting position, showing eye-focus position

Fig 8. The 'set' position

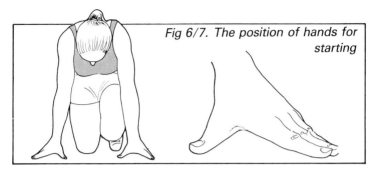

Fig 6/7. The position of hands for
starting

Looking again at figure 5, you see a medium start position, shoulders over the hands, which are in a high tripod, shoulder width apart (see figures 6 and 7).

Block angles
The angle of the front block should be shallow and that of the back block steep. This allows the ankles to work at their best angle, 90°.

Hands and shoulders
From the front, the start position should show the hands shoulder width apart (see figure 6/7). This gives a direct, linear arm-thrust on the report of the gun. Looking from the side, the shoulders should be directly above the hands. From this position there is only one movement — a lift of the hips, on the command 'set'. You must avoid any forward/upward movement which, if it is less than precise, can put tension on the shoulders.

The 'set' position
This is simple! Lift the hips above shoulder level, with your back flat. This produces a 90° bend of the front leg, which is essential to a good, rangy block thrust (see figure 8). The back leg, whose job is to give a short 'dig' off the blocks, has a shallow angle. There must be pressure on the back block, or block velocity will suffer.

Head position
Keep your head in line with the spine, looking about 1 metre ahead (see figure 5). This eye-focus is critical — if the head lifts on the gun report, the trunk will simply come up with it, producing poor block velocity.

Gun reaction
Reaction practices are detailed on page 44. Remember the correct feeling — that of not reacting to the gun, but being released by it. To this end, there is no substitute for regular start practice to the gun, preferably in competitive situations; you cannot effectively simulate starting without competition.

The pick-up
It is the quality of the pick-up which makes a great starter.
The 'feel' of good starting is of rangy block thrust, of long
block contact. I used to ask sprinters to imagine that
someone had nailed their launching foot to the block! That is
really the feeling to achieve, and this should be the feeling to
achieve, and this should be the feeling through the pick-up
— cling, cling, cling. The action to aim for is that of a low,
flat trunk, with big leg-extension.

The best possible training for pick-up of the highest quality
is to add elbow-drive (page 39) and knee pick-up to the basic
start drills. It is important to drill the start and pick-up,
working on one section at a time. Without 'movement feel',
without sensitivity, you can learn very little and only when
you have a movement vocabulary (a verbal expression of the
actions you need) do you get reference points to which you
can return when problems arise.

The middle of the race

At the beginning of the race there is a lot of ground contact
time — some 0.12 seconds and above. This high force factor
diminishes as the race progresses, and then the 'feel' to go
for must be of flow. It is here that all the running drills pay
off. The essence of running — the still head and shoulders,
legs pumping fluently and powerfully below the trunk and the
arms working strongly and directly about it — now comes
into play. At this stage you must let everything flow — really
let it pour!

The finish

More finishes are lost than won. By this I mean that there are
several pit-falls which can lose you the race — tightening up
under pressure in mid race, trying harder over the final 20-30
metres, or making an early dip for the tape. Instead,
remember that what wins races are the following:

1 Holding form
2 'Lifting' into the finish; run tall
3 Dipping late, in the final stride
4 'Blocking' — that is feeling that the focus of your
attention is the 'tunnel' of the lane.

You can practise all these in training, using isolation drills or
race situations. Indeed, there is nothing that cannot be
practised or simulated effectively in training. Appropriate
isolation drills are listed on pages 36-45.

400 metres — a different race

Sprinters who run the 400-metre distance move on to a different energy system from that employed by the 100- and 200-metre runners (see table, page 11). Because of this, they must not only have speed, but also a special kind of endurance — speed-endurance. This means that they cannot rely on the short-term (5-6 seconds) anaerobic energy, but must move on to aerobic energy. Unfortunately, in delivering this energy, glycogen produces lactic acid, the by-products of which interfere with muscle contraction. When a television commentator describes a 400-metre runner as 'wallowing in a sea of lactic acid', this is not strictly true, but it is accurate enough to serve our purpose.

The difference between 100- and 200-metre athletes and the 400-metre man is that the 400-metre runner is a speed-endurance animal. Most male world-class one-lap specialists can run 100 metres in 10.50 seconds or under, with ladies running in the 11.0-11.4 second range. More importantly, the men can usually run around 20.50 for the 200 metres and the ladies around 22.2. Though basic speed is essential, the 200 metres emerges as a much better guide to a runner's 400-metre potential than the short sprint. The type for 400-metre racing is more a Carl Lewis than a Ben Johnson.

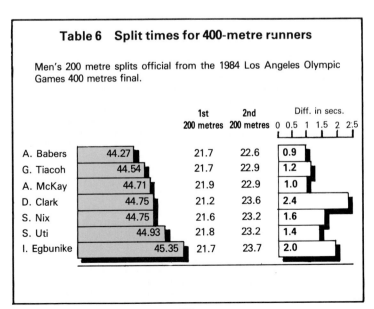

Table 6   Split times for 400-metre runners

Men's 200 metre splits official from the 1984 Los Angeles Olympic Games 400 metres final.

	1st 200 metres	2nd 200 metres	Diff. in secs.
A. Babers	44.27	21.7	22.6	0.9
G. Tiacoh	44.54	21.7	22.9	1.2
A. McKay	44.71	21.9	22.9	1.0
D. Clark	44.75	21.2	23.6	2.4
S. Nix	44.75	21.6	23.2	1.6
S. Uti	44.93	21.8	23.2	1.4
I. Egbunike	45.35	21.7	23.7	2.0

400 metre break-down

Just as the 200 metres is not really a flat-out sprint, so the 400 metres is not simply 200 metres of sprinting followed by 200 metres of slow death. It is in the ability to balance the first and second 200-metre stretches that races are either won or lost.

Table 6 (see page 27) shows the final of the men's 400 metres in the 1984 Los Angeles Olympics, we see that Babers (USA) ran these stretches in 21.7 and 22.6 seconds respectively, showing a differential of 0.9 seconds. Throughout the seven finalists, only a couple of metres spanned six of them at the half-way point, the exception being Darren Clark (Australia) who blasted out to 21.2 seconds to take a 4-metre lead.

From the differentials between Clark's first and second 200 metres, it seems that he fell apart in the second section of the race (23.6 seconds) with a 2.4-second differential. There is no telling what his differential would have been had he run, say, a more cautious 21.7 seconds for the first part of the race, but if he could then have managed even a final 22.9 seconds, he would have found himself in a medal position. In the first three positions, the average differential is just over 1.0 second. The next four average 1.8 seconds.

Even the fastest of short sprinters often have difficulty in moving up to the one-lap race. Conversely, 200-metre runners who are a few tenths slower, often find that they have the ability to adapt to the longer distance or, more importantly, they can readily take on the severity of 400-metre training.

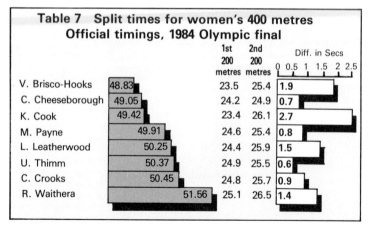

Table 7   Split times for women's 400 metres
Official timings, 1984 Olympic final

	1st 200 metres	2nd 200 metres	Diff. in Secs
V. Brisco-Hooks	48.83	23.5	25.4	1.9
C. Cheeseborough	49.05	24.2	24.9	0.7
K. Cook	49.42	23.4	26.1	2.7
M. Payne	49.91	24.6	25.4	0.8
L. Leatherwood	50.25	24.4	25.9	1.5
U. Thimm	50.37	24.9	25.5	0.6
C. Crooks	50.45	24.8	25.7	0.9
R. Waithera	51.56	25.1	26.5	1.4

Race tactics

Take a look at the race in more detail. At a beginner's level, the aim should simply be to stride the whole distance, keeping an even effort-level and maintaining good form all the way. With beginners there is no room for any sophisticated ideas — the aim is to avoid, on the one hand, a 'sprint and die' approach, and on the other, a slow slog over the first half which leaves the runner too much to do in the second part of the race. The most common error with novices is the 'sprint and die' syndrome — as beginners usually have no idea of effort levels. This is where the sprint drills can help by giving the runner 'feel' for different levels of effort. It is this ability to 'read' your own body which is central to developing skill at all levels of performance.

At higher levels of performance, this simplistic approach is not sufficient. Here the start is, first, a driving action — but not the full-blooded drive of 100-metre sprinting. The 'feel' is more a 'flow-drive'. The aim is to 'lock in' to the effort level at which you are going to run the first part of the race — and you achieve this in the first 100 metres of the race.

The second 100-200 metres section must be treated as a unit. If in this section you find that the field is getting away from you, you may have to react by quickening the pulse of your running, by 'lifting' slightly as in the short sprints. Such reactions must still be only marginal in nature. If you adjust too substantially, then changes are often uneconomical and probably unrealistic. The best runners move into their 'effort groove' from the gun, and any reactive activity tends to take place in the third 100 metres of the race.

This consideration allows the best one-lap runners to have 'kick reserve' in the final straight, while others, even if they are in challenging positions, are merely hanging on.

It requires great skill, great sensitivity to run on the edge of fatigue, just managing to keep sufficient reserve to ensure that the final straight is not flat-footed agony. That must be the aim of the 400-metre runner. The roots of success lie in these requirements:

● Good running technique through drills
● Simulation practices, putting technique under pressure
● Developing sensitivity to your body, both in training and racing, going for a 'feel' just as with shorter sprints

All of these are, of course, placed against a background of solid body-conditioning.

29

Relays

The essence of winning relay running is a clean exchange which matches the speeds of incoming and outgoing runners. A runner like Linford Christie will surge into the exchange zone at around 42 k.p.h., decelerating slightly as fatigue sets in. If he were to hand the baton over at the first legal point (10 metres) the outgoing runner is unlikely to be running at much better than 26-29 k.p.h! However, at the 26 metre point, the outgoing runner is possibly running at 37-40 k.p.h. and the speed loss is therefore minimal. It is in this area that the exchange should be made for, although 2 metres later (28 metres) would involve even less loss of speed, it would not offer a sufficient margin of safety.

Selection
Speed matching is central to relay racing. This can be achieved using different methods of exchange, so the nature of the runners must dictate the method of exchange. The aim throughout is baton-speed.

Leaving aside each athlete's baton-handling abilities, as a general rule, a fast-starting curve-runner is important for the first stage, and a runner with good speed-endurance is valuable on the second leg. On the third stage, speed-endurance and curve-running are important — a good 200-metre runner can be invaluable. The fourth leg requires no curve-running ability, but rather good speed-endurance and ability to hold fast under pressure.

Methods of exchange
Central to all methods of exchange is concept of *free distance* — that is, the difference made by the length of the extended

Fig 9. The relay exchange zone, showing optimum area to hand the baton.

	Best exchange area	Acceptable but not good

← 20m →

The shaded area beyond the mid-point of the exchange-point of the exchange-zone, preferably in the final four metres, ensures the best speed-match of incoming and outgoing runners.

arm and baton. To take a ridiculous example, imagine that the baton is of the length of a vaulting-pole — the exchange could take place early at a speed of 40 k.p.h, when the incoming runner was at the 200-metre mark and the outgoing runner at the 25-metre mark. The upsweep and downsweep methods (see figures 10 and 11) show the more modest but practicable gains which can be made by the downsweep method. More importantly, it shows that, by having both arms close to extension, you can make early exchanges, producing a modest 'vaulting pole' effect. Free distance is therefore another factor affecting baton speed.

Many international teams use the upsweep method, with a right-left-right-left sequence, so that there is no loss of speed in changing the baton from one hand to another. (This sequence means the baton goes from athlete 1's right hand to athlete 2's left hand, and so on.) However, there is no doubt that the downsweep, properly executed, has two advantages:

● Greater 'free distance' (compare figures 10 and 11).
● No 'baton shrinkage' — this is when the outgoing runner receives only the tip of the baton rather than the full length — and no adjustment during running, as the baton is handed on in such a manner that the outgoing runner has it immediately in the position in which it has to be handed on to the next outgoing runner.

The difficulty with this method is that, if an error is made and an incoming runner over-runs his partner, a downsweep exchange is difficult to execute. There is also often a tendency for the incoming runner to go into a slow-motion 'hang' in making the exchange.

Lane positioning and starting
In a right-left-right-left sequence of exchange, the second runner will stand on the right of his lane, the third on the left of his lane, and the fourth on the right of his lane.

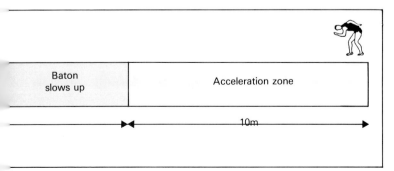

Baton slows up	Acceleration zone

10m

The reason for this is simple. Relay racing is the one event in which two athletes share a lane; the outgoing runner simply leaves space for his partner to run in to make the exchange at full speed. This avoids the twisting and consequent loss of speed which would occur if the two runners exchanged with one directly behind the other.

Figure 12 shows a runner using a semi-crouch position, left foot forward, looking over her right shoulder at the incoming runner. This foot placement allows good vision of the incoming runner with minimum twisting.

The other alternative is the one-hand start (figure 13) which gives greater stability. As in a standard crouch-start, the hand is in line with the mid line of the body to give a greater balance.

Check marks

The knack central to good exchanges is having accurate check marks, using marker tape. These check marks must be worked out by trial and error. The major problem in establishing accurate check marks is the unwillingness of sprinters to run flat out over the full race distance in training. Runs over 40-80 metres are fine for establishing the outgoing runner's ability to run out explosively as the incoming runner's

Fig 10. The upsweep baton exchange

Fig 11. The downsweep baton exchange

hips cross the check mark and for assessing his ability to put back a still 'target' hand on his partner's shout. What they do not show is the relationship between the outgoing runner and a possibly fading incoming runner over the full competition distance.

It is therefore essential that you have a couple of runs over the full distance in practice, so that accurate and realistic check marks can be established.

Exchange

Most international teams use a 'shout' exchange, in which the incoming runner shouts 'hand' when he is a stride away from his partner and he sweeps the baton strongly up into his partner's hand.

The shout 'hand' must be loud and decisive, as there is a great deal of noise in the exchange area. This must be immediately followed by a strong sweep-up into the outgoing runner's hand, so that the exchange takes place within two strides of the shout. The arm should be almost fully extended and the hand should form a wide, downward 'V', with palm stretched. It is essential to stretch the hand, so that it provides a large target for the incoming runner. It is also vital that the outgoing runner receives the maximum baton length,

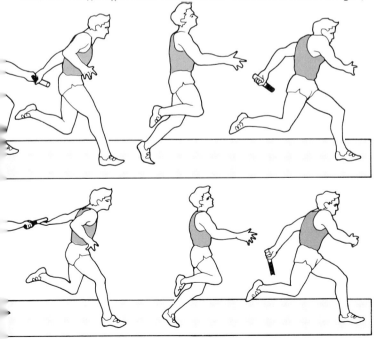

rather than merely the tip of the baton, in order that he is not forced to make adjustments during running.

It is equally vital that the outgoing runner does not 'tread water' as his partner approaches him, for if the check mark is correct, the connection will be made in the 24-26-metre area. He must drive out strongly and with confidence as he would in a sprint race. Similarly, there must be no 'hanging' or subconscious tensing and holding back by the incoming runner, anticipating the exchange.

Competition wise

In relays there is often a big gap between training and competition. This is usually because training practices have mainly been over short distances. Although this can produce slick baton-changing, it often results in a poor correlation between training and competitive check marks.

Even when there has been adequate training over competition distances, there is often a change in competition conditions, simply because the outgoing runner is too cautious and either moves in his check mark or goes out too slowly on the correct check mark. In either case, he is over-run early in the zone with consequent loss of baton-speed.

Another problem, particularly in major competition, is that an inexperienced runner panics and goes out too early, or produces a higher zone-speed than he has ever shown in training. This results in a 'foul' or an inevitable slowing down to a trot to receive the baton inside the exchange zone.

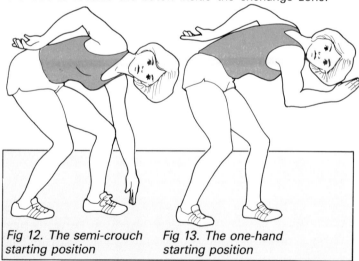

Fig 12. The semi-crouch starting position

Fig 13. The one-hand starting position

Finally, check-mark distances (which should be measured in foot-lengths) should be modified to take into account prevailing conditions. For instance, a check mark for the second exchange might need to be taken in by two foot-lengths to accommodate a 4-metres-per-second head-wind on the back straight. Similarly, a 2-metres-per-second back-wind on the curve at the final exchange might mean adding a foot-length. Here are some suggested practices:

Relay training schedules

1 Baton practice (standing).
Runners stand 'forces-style' in line and on the shout 'hand', put back their hands, one at a time, in a stretched 'V', arm almost straight. Practise this with both hands.

2 Baton practice (standing, pairs).
As for practice 1, with partner shouting 'hand', and placing the baton in the extended hand.

3 Baton practice (jogging, pairs).
As for practice 2, at jogging speed, then with slow strides.

4 For the outgoing runner (ability to go out on check mark and to run out at speed).
Incoming runner runs 60 metres without the baton. The test is whether or not the outgoing runner can go out consistently on the incoming runner's hips crossing the check mark.

5 For the outgoing runner (ability to go out on check mark and to run out at speed).
As for practice 4, the priority being the strong drive-out through the zone. Speed-matching can be assessed and check marks adjusted if there is over-running (lengthen check mark), or failure to reach (shorten check mark).

6 For the outgoing runner (ability to go out on check mark and to run out at speed with baton).
Here the aim is to see if it all works — a clean, fast exchange made within two strides of the shout 'hand'. There are several possible errors, so it is best to station other runners at the check point as well as the exchange point. The main errors are either going out too late or too early, or going out too slowly. The tendency is to over-run, often a combination of going out late and slow.

7 As for practice 6, over the full distance, with the outgoing runner continuing to run 40 metres beyond the exchange zone.
This is the same practice as 6, over the full distance. Key points are a) going out on the check mark and b) strong running out. Now, at full distance, it is also worth checking on the speed maintenance of the incoming runner. It often helps to make this practice competitive by filling inside and outside lanes, for greater realism.

CHAPTER SEVEN

Isolation drills

Martha Graham once said 'Technique is freedom' — and
certainly it is the means by which an athlete can apply force
effectively. Bad technique is like a leaky bucket — the power
pours in but seeps through the leaks and consequently speed
is lost.

Running drills aim to focus effort into effective movement
so that, in 'Star Wars' terms 'the force is with you' and you
are not struggling against yourself. The objective is to make
power seem effortless, fluent. Everyone has had a moment
when they performed a feat of physical skill at the highest
level — the feeling after is 'It felt easy', or 'I felt as if I wasn't
trying'. That is the sensation Florence Griffith-Joyner must
have as she pours effortlessly past the winning post, way
ahead of the field.

In the very best of performers, these movements are not a
matter of chance, but are rather the result of thousands of
hours of mental and physical preparation. The drills which
follow have both a physical and psychological element, the
two of which are inextricably linked.

Properly performed, these drills can produce a fluid,
mechanical sprinting technique, and from there, I can
guarantee an improvement in speed too. It is a matter of
teaching your muscles to act in a skilful manner — and at the
heart of good technique is a still trunk and head, arms
working rhythmically and fluently about the trunk, the legs
flowing effortlessly (see figure 6).

The overall impression is of ease and grace. Some runners
do this fairly well from the beginning, but most do not, and
even the best can, using drills, make those minute
improvements, shave off hundredths of a second and make
the difference between winning and losing when a race is
closely contested.

The drills

Carry out all drills (except 'driving practice') over a minimum
distance of 40 metres. This is not any magic distance — it is
simply that any shorter distance does not give enough time
for you to feel the rhythm of the run. Most fit athletes prefer
runs of about 60 metres, performed in sets of four per drill,
allowing a couple of minutes' rest between sets.

1 Head and trunk drill

Jog into the start on the balls of the feet, hips high. Stride at 80% of maximum effort, keeping your shoulders low, arms moving loosely back and forwards at right angles (see figure 14).

This 'fix' of low shoulders and still head and trunk is central to all good running. Any hunching of the shoulders or wobbling of the head causes a loss of running line and causes tension and consequent fatigue.

The 'feel' — imagine a pin driven in at shoulder level, with arms rotating loosely about that pin, like a doll (see figure 15).

Fig 14. Low-shouldered relaxed position

Fig 15. Head and trunk posture, as if with a pin through the shoulders

2 'Potato crisp' drill

Drill No 1 is general, focussing on broad, overall movements; its aim is to give the 'big picture' of sprinting — the posture. This second drill looks at specific details which, if refined, produce a smooth and silky running technique.

Jog in on the start line with high hips, on the balls of the feet. Form your thumb and index finger into a rectangle (see figure 16), keeping the wrists relaxed. Imagine you are holding a potato crisp between thumb and index finger. Run at 80% effort, stressing the hand/wrist relaxation.

The 'feel' is an immediate flow of relaxation through the body, coming from the relaxation of the hands.

Fig 17. The hand-fix drill position

Fig 16. 'Potato crisp' relaxed hand position

3   Hand-fix drill

The aim of this drill is to fix the forward movement of hand and lower arm. The upper arm should stay flabby (see figure 17) — ensure that the hand goes no higher than shoulder height and to the body mid-line. A common error is to pump the hands upwards, well beyond the shoulder-line or across the body, as this makes the shoulders lift or rotate.

4   Elbow drive drill

If you watch any great sprinter, you can see that the hands are not simply lifted in front to shoulder level, but work backwards, through a good range of movement. This drill keeps the shoulders still, improves the thrust of the arms and, as a consequence, the drive of the legs.

The 'feel' is a focus on driving the elbows back, as you run, checking the hand at hip height.

Fig 18. The elbow drive position

5   Arm impulse drill

This is partly a test of relaxed arm action, and you need to focus on this one aspect of your movement. Jog in on the start line, then gradually increase the force of the arm action throughout the run.

The 'feel' is of added impulse, a steady but almost effortless increase in speed.

6 'Jelly jaw' drill

This is a drill which gets the most laughs — it is also one of the few which the coach can demonstrate in person!

When you see world-class sprinters running at their best, you notice the relaxation in the head and neck — Carl Lewis is a perfect example. Any tension in this area is lethal, as it transfers down the spine to the working muscles and causes loss of speed — no muscle, after all, is isolated. Running power has to come from a fine and correct balance between

Fig 19. 'Jelly jaw' position

tension and relaxation, and when you get this balance, sprinting is a pure and unalloyed flowing action.

Jog in on the start, consciously allowing your jaw and facial muscles to relax. Hit your run at 80% effort, allowing your jaw to hang loose — literally, getting the 'jelly jaw' effect.

Fig 20. Leg speed drill

The next stage is to put 'jelly jaw' under pressure at higher speeds. Run 30 metres at 80% effort, then raise this to 90-100%, still trying to maintain head and neck relaxation.

The 'feel' is of overall relaxation and flowing with a consciousness of your face being 'wobbly' and mobile.

7   Driving practice drill
Adopt the standing-start position, toes forward, hip width apart, your back flat, head in line with the spine with a forward lean. Run out, stressing the sensation of holding the driving foot on the ground. The foot must not leave the ground until the leg is fully extended!

Make these runs over 30 metres, preferably in spikes and on an artificial surface. You can practise in a gym, using warm-up shoes, but full leg-extension is harder to achieve on a wooden surface and in a less supple warm-up shoe. Initially the drill will feel slow, even ponderous, but this will change as you find balance and control. To take the drill further, try the following refinements:

● Keep your eyes focussed on the ground ahead — this will prevent your trunk from lifting too soon
● Add elbow drive (see drill 4)
● Next, add high knee pick-up (see drill 9)

Work on six repetitions of the basic exercise, then take two minutes' rest before adding repetitions. Work on only one element at a time.

The 'feel' is of cling, cling, cling — keeping ground-contact. This is the element of the drill which needs most attention.

8   Leg-speed drill
Sprinting is a combination of stride-length and leg-speed (see figure 20). There is no point in having a 3-metre long stride if your strike-rate is only two per second. Conversely you'll never achieve any great speed by moving your legs like a fiddler's elbow if you only cover 1 metre at each stride.

Jog in on the start then hit 80% effort level, stressing an increase in leg-cadence. It may help to emphasise speed of arm action, but remember that the aim is not a crab-like, running-on-the-spot action. What you must aim for is a marginal quickening of running pulse.

The 'feel' of leg speed is best achieved by making a 30-metre run without stress on leg speed, then flowing into a 30-metre stretch of leg speed.

9 High knee pick-up drill

Good range of movement is vital in sprinting — Linford
Christie clearly shows an excellent knee pick-up. Many factors
go to produce this, including strong abdominals and hip
flexors, plus co-ordinated relaxation of the muscles of the
back of the thigh. It also comes from a muscular learning
process, because mere strength or suppleness, though it
provides the basis for skill, does not automatically produce
the skill itself.

Jog in with a high knee action, trunk vertical, then flow on
into an 80% effort stride, trying to hold the high knee pick-up
action (see figure 21). You would never be able to hold the
knees at the same height during the run itself, but the aim is
to minimize loss of height.

The 'feel' is of a fixed trunk — you must not lean back or
you will produce a false knee pick-up and a prancing,
backwards action.

Fig 21. High knee
pick-up drill

10 Lift drill

This is a variation on the high knee pick-up drill, and
sometimes produces better results. It relates directly to the
'lifting' action used by top sprinters over the final 20-30
metres of a race.

Run 30 metres at 80-90% effort, then run the final 30
metres, stressing a lift of the knees and chest.

The 'feel' to go for is that of a high pumping action.

11 Lower leg drill

The aim is to ensure that the lower leg lands actively, so minimizing any braking action on each ground contact. This is a subtle practice — leave it until you have mastered the 'bread and butter' drills. If you link it up with leg-speed practices, results can be excellent.

Practise almost on the spot at first (see figure 22), with high knees, aiming to produce a flailing 'out and back' action. (This will look nothing like running and give more of an impression of a high-stepping trotting pony.) Don't lean back!

The next step is to feed this movement into your running action. Jog in and move to 80% effort level, but with particular stress on high leg-speed, your lower leg moving actively under your trunk.

The 'feel', if you are getting it right, is of fluency and continuity, of legs pouring under the hips. Remember to keep your leg-speed high (see figures 23a and 23b).

Fig 22. Lower leg drill

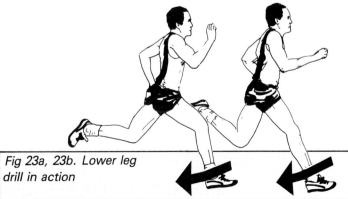

Fig 23a, 23b. Lower leg drill in action

12   Reaction drill

Until Ben Johnson's victory in the Rome 1987 World
Championships, little attention was paid to reaction time —
that is, the gap between the firing of the starting pistol and
the first movement of the body, in the case of sprinting, the
exertion of pressure on the back block. (See table 8 for
timings.)

For the drill, carry out regular starting practice, to the gun,
in scratch races over 40-60 metres, then in handicap races
over the same distance.

Further improvement comes from
● Thinking of the gun as an inevitable release.
● Balance on the blocks.
● A fixed breathing routine in the 'set' gun period. Take
an inward breath on 'set' with relaxed exhalation on the gun.
This links well with the sense of release.

The 'feel' will come only if you think of the report of the gun
as part of a flowing sequence, which allows you to surge out
from the blocks, not as a separate sound.

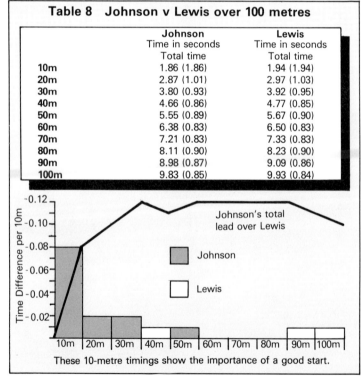

Table 8   Johnson v Lewis over 100 metres

	Johnson Time in seconds Total time	Lewis Time in seconds Total time
10m	1.86 (1.86)	1.94 (1.94)
20m	2.87 (1.01)	2.97 (1.03)
30m	3.80 (0.93)	3.92 (0.95)
40m	4.66 (0.86)	4.77 (0.85)
50m	5.55 (0.89)	5.67 (0.90)
60m	6.38 (0.83)	6.50 (0.83)
70m	7.21 (0.83)	7.33 (0.83)
80m	8.11 (0.90)	8.23 (0.90)
90m	8.98 (0.87)	9.09 (0.86)
100m	9.83 (0.85)	9.93 (0.84)

Johnson's total lead over Lewis

Johnson

Lewis

These 10-metre timings show the importance of a good start.

13   Blocking drill

Sprinting is simply eight men running up eight tubes, through eight tunnels of space, destroying that space with the velocity of their movements. The less the sprinter relates to what is happening on each side of him, the better. Unlike the distance-runner, he can do nothing about events around him, so blocking is essential to shut out useless and potentially damaging information.

This is a step beyond technique, beyond 'jelly jaw' and 'potato crisps', into the essence of any closed skill — its accurate reproduction, independent of the distractions of the environment. The aim is to run up your lane seeing nothing but 4 feet of space.

The 'feel', when you get it right, is that of completely blocking all other events and irrelevant details around you — you have the feeling of surging through the 'tunnel' which is your lane.

14   Curve drills

Curve running is an element which most affects 200-metre running. Technically, the 200 metres is a sprint, yet any sprinter knows that blasting the first 60 metres then attempting to hang on is pure kamikaze. This is because of the curve itself, which places restrictions on speed, and because such tactics would involve a large loss of speed in the last part of the race.

The aim is to find a fine balance of 95-98% effort which enables the sprinter to come out of the curve running high and loose. At international level, the curve is run in about 10.7 seconds, and the final 100 metres in around 9.2-9.6 seconds.

Run at 80-90% effort, stressing:

- a dropping of the inside arm
- a slight cross-action of the outside arm
- high leg-speed
- a 'lift' out of the curve (see drill 10)

Practise each of these separately, then put them into the whole action. They should come together in the final two runs, which need to be over at least 130 metres in order to practise the 'lift' out of the curve.

CHAPTER EIGHT

Middle-distance running

Sprint events are the only ones which involve 'pure' speed and no other elements. Distance-running is, by its nature, mostly aerobic (see table 3), moving from 60-40% anaerobic/aerobic ratio at 800 metres to one of 2/98% in the marathon. There is therefore virtually no requirement for sprinting speed in marathon running, as even the 2% of anaerobic activity does not reflect a sprint, but rather the build-up of waste products in the final part of the race as the runner moves into the anaerobic state.

It is only really in the middle distances (800 and 1500 metres) that sheer sprinting speed assumes importance, for it is impossible for a world-class 800-metre runner to run inside 1 minute 44 seconds without chalking up 400 metres in under 49 seconds. This, in turn, means registering about 22.5-23.0 seconds for the 200 metres and a timing of 11.2-11.5 seconds for the 100 metres.

A fair turn of speed, added to basic endurance, means that the 800-metre runner can 'cruise' when the bell clangs at 50.4 seconds, with plenty of reserve in hand to cover any breaks down the back straight. There is no way by which a runner whose 400-metre best is, say, 50.0 seconds, can be anywhere in contention at such speeds. If he does try to hang in close to the leaders, he will find a massive lactic acid build-up at around 600 metres and a 'DOA' (dead on arrival) situation in the home straight!

Similarly, in a slow race, the runner with good sprint speed will be able to 'kick' in a final 100 metres in below 12 seconds, and stride a fast final furlong because of his reserves of speed.

There are different types of speed required in middle-distance. 'Kicking' speed — the ability to surge away from the field within a few metres (Steve Ovett in the late 70s was one of the most powerful 'kickers' of this type) — is different from the slower 'winding up' speed of runners such as Peter Elliott or Steve Cram who, because of their lack of basic leg-power, always prefer to make their hits over a longer distance. Sebastian Coe like Ovett, had the capacity to kick suddenly, creating lethal 5-metre gaps, even against powerful rivals. At his peak, Coe's basic speed (11.0, 21.8 and 46.5 seconds over 100, 200 and 400 metres respectively) gave him immense

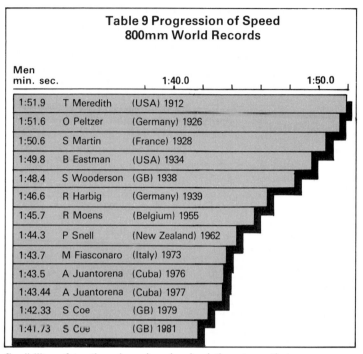

**Table 9 Progression of Speed
800mm World Records**

Men min. sec.			1:40.0				1:50.0
1:51.9	T Meredith	(USA) 1912					
1:51.6	O Peltzer	(Germany) 1926					
1:50.6	S Martin	(France) 1928					
1:49.8	B Eastman	(USA) 1934					
1:48.4	S Wooderson	(GB) 1938					
1:46.6	R Harbig	(Germany) 1939					
1:45.7	R Moens	(Belgium) 1955					
1:44.3	P Snell	(New Zealand) 1962					
1:43.7	M Fiasconaro	(Italy) 1973					
1:43.5	A Juantorena	(Cuba) 1976					
1:43.44	A Juantorena	(Cuba) 1977					
1:42.33	S Coe	(GB) 1979					
1:41.73	S Coe	(GB) 1981					

flexibility of tactics since he also had the strength to cover breaks from a long way out easily, and could kick from almost any distance. If Coe stayed close to the leaders into the final straight in a slow race, the other runners knew that they were in big trouble. Said Aouita, the 1988 Olympic 5000 metre champion, was unusual in that he had immense ability in the 400 metres (46.8 seconds) and 800 metres (1 minute 43.4 seconds), which gave him a speed-reserve in 5000 metres and 10,000 metres, although these are essentially aerobic events. Aouita's combination of speed and endurance over such a range of distances is unique and devastating.

How much speed does a distance-runner need? Certainly the basic essentials — the 'feel' of sprinting, for the sprint action is a different skill from that of even-paced distance-running, and this can be learned from sprint drills (see page 22). Unless, like Coe and Ovett, the middle-distance runner has outstanding natural speed, he will be confined to two possible tactical approaches. One involves fast, even-paced running; the other depends on slow wind-ups of speed from a long way out. Both methods can be effective, but they are painful and can sometimes be covered by other runners slipstreaming in the wake of the leader.

Speed drills

Carry out these speed drills once a week throughout the
season (for a distance-runner 1000 metres of speed drills
means little more than a warm-up) and at 80% effort level.
The distance-runner must learn to work in different gears, and
develop sensitivity in his body to the feel of different speed
and effort levels.

1 6 × 150 metres   First 50 metres at stride-level (80%
effort); second 50 metres slow, 'winding up' acceleration;
final 50 metres, 'hit' using elbow drive up to 100% effort.

2 4 × 200 metres   First 100 metres slow acceleration to
90% effort, then a sudden 'hit' with stress on leg-speed to
100% effort in the final 100 metres.

Fig 24. The centre of gravity stays as level as possible

3 4 × 300 metres Run 200 metres at 80% effort. In the final 100 metres, accelerate all the way into the tape — 'building, building, building' — stressing the feel of 'running tall'.

4 3 × 400 metres Run 200 metres at 80% effort. Kick at 200 metres to 100%, holding form all the way into the tape.

5 2 × 600 metres Run 400 at 800-metres race pace, kick on leg-speed at 200 metres to 100% effort.

Exercises 1, 2 and 3 are virtually fatigue-free practices — almost pure sprinting, while 4 and 5 put the sprint technique under stress, simulating race situations. It is best to perform the latter practices with partners, switching 'race roles' in each run. Best of all, work within a group, so that you can get the 'feel' of working amongst bobbing elbows and knees,

finding yourself space, and under fatigue conditions.

Remember, by constant, slow aerobic running, distance-runners often kill whatever basic speed they have and actually 'learn' to be slow runners! You must set out deliberately to learn speed, so as not to lose a vital and winning weapon in your racing armoury.

Speed cannot, however, be separated from other elements such as upper-body strength and leg-resilience. The distance-runner must use weight and circuit training (see pages 70 and 74) to develop a body which is totally strong, rather than simply a pair of legs with a head on top. Similarly, a programme of plyometrics (see page 76) will develop elastic strength which is particularly valuable in acceleration. Bearing in mind the time spent by many distance-runners in running itself (often over 12 hours a week), a couple of hours of speed and strength training is time well spent.

Middle-distance speed schedules

It is not only short-distance sprinters who need to cultivate the power to run fast. One of the biggest mistakes made by many middle-distance runners is segregating too rigidly their periods of long, slow distance ('LSD') running, strength-endurance and speed training. This can mean that the 'LSD' period often contains no strength-endurance or speed. When speed does make a late appearance towards the end of the training session (April to May), there is often injury, simply because the muscles are suddenly being asked to act in a different manner. Alternatively, the runner finds great difficulty in producing anything like a sprint technique because his system is deconditioned in sprinting terms.

The answer to this is to preserve a speed element throughout the whole winter conditioning period so that the skill of fast running is kept fresh in neuro-muscular terms. The best way to do this is to perform isolation drills, as described on pages 36 - 45. These, done at 80% effort, are little more than a warm-up of 1000-1500 metres for a middle-distance runner, who should go through them at least once a week during the winter months.

Once you reach the sharpening period, push up the speed of these drills. More importantly, practise speed under fatigue conditions, simulating the pressures of the race itself. The following are typical sessions:

1 4 × 600 metres at 90% effort, allowing almost complete recovery between runs. Run the first 400 metres at 80%

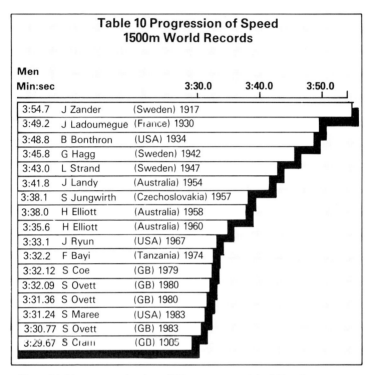

Table 10 Progression of Speed 1500m World Records

Min:sec		
3:54.7	J Zander	(Sweden) 1917
3:49.2	J Ladoumegue	(France) 1930
3:48.8	B Bonthron	(USA) 1934
3:45.8	G Hagg	(Sweden) 1942
3:43.0	L Strand	(Sweden) 1947
3:41.8	J Landy	(Australia) 1954
3:38.1	S Jungwirth	(Czechoslovakia) 1957
3:38.0	H Elliott	(Australia) 1958
3:35.6	H Elliott	(Australia) 1960
3:33.1	J Ryun	(USA) 1967
3:32.2	F Bayi	(Tanzania) 1974
3:32.12	S Coe	(GB) 1979
3:32.09	S Ovett	(GB) 1980
3:31.36	S Ovett	(GB) 1980
3:31.24	S Maree	(USA) 1983
3:30.77	S Ovett	(GB) 1983
3:29.67	S Cram	(GB) 1985

effort, kicking over the last 200 metres and holding form over the full distance.

2 6 × 400 metres at 90% effort, allowing almost complete recovery between runs. Kick at any distance from 200 metres to the finish.

3 3 × 800 metres at 90% effort, with 6 minutes between runs. Kick at 200 metres, then kick again at 50 metres from the finish.

4 8-10 × 300 metres at 90-95% effort, allowing almost complete recovery between runs, stressing relaxation and the feeling of 'flow' at gliding speed.

The aim is grace under pressure. When form falls apart, then it is time to stop. The most effective stimulation comes from work in groups, where you have to deal with the elbows and knees of real competition. Equally important, group-work lets you get used to finding effective positions from which to kick. This is where the sterile pace of time-trials often fails to correlate with racing itself. Remember, all training is running practice — but practice does not make perfect — rather it makes permanent.

CHAPTER NINE

Hurdles

It is massive over-simplification to say that hurdling is just sprinting over barriers. It is a specific and specialized skill which, though highly correlated with sprinting ability, is as different from sprinting as it is from the long jump. It is not the speed of approach to the first hurdle, nor is it pure sprinting speed which is crucial to hurdling — it is speed across and between the barriers.

You need to look at the technique in its entirety — both the speed element and the hurdle technique, which are inextricably linked. Certainly, to reach world class, a male hurdler must be able to run under 10.40 seconds for 100 metres and a female hurdler under 11.40 seonds. Reynaldo Nehemiah, one of two hurdlers to dip below 13.00 seconds, had an estimated flat speed over 110 metres of close to 11.10 seconds — giving a differential of about 1.90 seconds. Britain's best hurdler, Colin Jackson (13.11 seconds) runs closer to 11.30 seconds on the flat, showing, in fact, an even better differential of about 1.8 seconds. It emerges that the stride-adjustments required by a tall, fast hurdler such as Nehemiah actually place him at a disadvantage, despite his great speed over 100 metres.

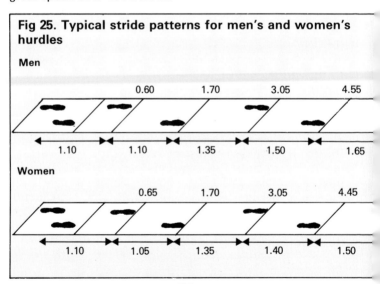

Fig 25. Typical stride patterns for men's and women's hurdles

Men

0.60   1.70   3.05   4.55

1.10   1.10   1.35   1.50   1.65

Women

0.65   1.70   3.05   4.45

1.10   1.05   1.35   1.40   1.50

Hurdling technique

The secret of hurdling lies in controlling to a minimum the rise and fall of the hurdler's centre of gravity (see figure 25). The more this flows on a flat path, the better — so this has a strong bearing on the posture you need for take-off at each hurdle.

What is less clear to many athletes is what happens in the first eight strides from the starting blocks into the first barrier. It is often there that the race is won or lost. A bad first hurdle, whether with too high a flight-path or hitting the hurdle, can lose that sudden half-metre of space — and perhaps just this short distance can make the difference between winning and losing.

The concept of 'running tall' is central to hurdling. This means keeping the centre of gravity as high as possible (the hips). This means the hurdler needs the minimum lift at each barrier — for example, if the hurdler runs in with a Groucho Marx scuttle, his centre of gravity is low, and this necessitates greater lift at each hurdle. This jumping action not only means more time is spent in the air, but also that the landing-leg has to absorb more shock. Over the full distance, this will increase the likelihood of the hurdler sinking lower and lower between barriers. In turn, this produces the need for a higher jump at each hurdle — so it goes from bad to worse, and Groucho becomes Sloucho!

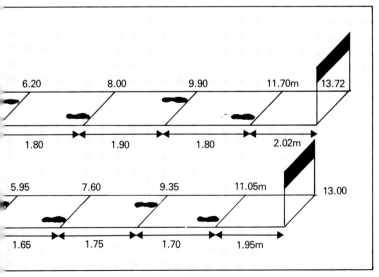

Fig 26. Fast thigh movement   Fig 27. The 'karate' elbow

Reaching the first hurdle

In men's hurdles there is a distance of 13.72 metres to the first hurdle, for women, 13 metres. In almost all cases, this takes eight strides, with a distance of 1.90-2.02 metres between take-off and hurdle.

If hurdling were just sprinting, then the hurdlers would simply power away from the blocks, hit the take-off spot and launch themselves at the barriers. Alas, hurdling is not that simple. Top-class male hurdlers vary from 1.83-1.90 metres in height, with relative differentials in leg-length. Natural sprinting has to be modified considerably, particularly for taller hurdlers.

Some hurdlers, finding that eight strides brings them too close to the barriers, opt for seven (this is less true of women, probably because the 13 metres into the first hurdle in the women's event more accurately reflects a woman's natural running). The problem with seven strides is that, if the hurdler is slightly below par, or if he is running into a stiff head-wind, then he may find himself struggling to reach the first hurdle. There is also the problem of a slower rhythm, one quite different from the high-cadence action between the hurdles.

So, for most runners, it is eight strides to the first hurdle. To accommodate this, two things can be done:
1 Block adjustments A normal sprint-start block position may not be appropriate, because it may bring the hurdler too far up the track on the first strides. Placing the blocks slightly

Fig 28. Piercing the space across the hurdle

Fig 29. An active split away from the hurdle

further back and/or bringing them closer together will give first strides appropriate to the first eight strides of the race. This is essentially a matter of trial and error.

2 High leg-speed An eight-stride approach is unnatural, each stride almost always shorter than the hurdler's natural stride length (figure 25 shows a typical stride-pattern for both male and female hurdlers). To deal with this, the aim must be to hit a rhythm immediately from the blocks — one which will be maintained throughout the race. There is no point in having four rangy strides, followed by four chopped ones — or six short strides preceding two enormous Beamonesque leaps into the hurdle.

Drill this rhythm until it becomes totally automatic, for until the hurdler can hit the take-off spot in balance, it is difficult to produce good horizontal velocity across the hurdle — and that is what hurdling is about — horizontal velocity. A high-hipped, on-the-balls-of-the-feet action must be central to all technical drills. Aim to run tall, with fast, high-cadence legs.

Although block adjustments are simply a matter of modifying equipment, or body-position on the equipment itself, the running action into the first hurdle is not.

The aim in all running practices is to develop the 'feel' — a sensitivity both to the body's movements and to the relationship between hurdle and hurdler. This sensory development is essential for every event, because it produces reference points — a body-language to which the hurdler can keep returning.

Taking the hurdle

You have reached the first hurdle, at high speed and in balance, with hips high, and you have hit the correct take-off point. Now you have got to increase speed through and away from the hurdle, driving horizontally across and off it.

The throw of a fast lead knee and the opposite arm and shoulder are simultaneous (see sequence, figure 26). Of the two, the vicious pick-up of the lead thigh is initially the more important, but it is essential that the actions are linked.

The 'feel' words are:

● 'Fast thigh!' (figure 26)

● 'Throw' the opposite shoulder at the hurdle, with karate elbow! (figure 27)

● 'Pierce' the space across the hurdle with your trunk. (figure 28)

● Make an active 'split away' from your driving leg on take off. (figure 29)

● Keep a continuous 'flowing' action with both legs.

The 'fast thigh' and 'opposite shoulder' throw are the vital keys to setting up a flat, fast movement across the hurdle, as they provide both the flight-path and the pace of the movement across the barrier. You need to drill these until they are completely automatic.

Similarly, the karate-like lower-leg movement is critical to a flat, fast clearance — a bent lower leg will necessitate a jumping action. Practise this away from the hurdle. The 'feel' is of throwing a fast heel at the barrier to produce a whippy, flailing action.

What photographs and diagrams cannot show is the horizontal thrust of the hurdler or the speed with which he comes off the hurdle. These following points are central to speed off the hurdle:

● Forward trunk pressure on top of the barrier (see figure 30). This means that on landing, the contact foot will not be ahead of the trunk. If it was, it would have a braking effect.

● A reaching action by the leading leg (see figure 32), so that it lands straight, producing a fast, pivot action.

● A strong 'down and back' action of the lead leg, so that the movement off the hurdle is active (see figure 32).

Athletes respond differently to the same verbal stimuli. It is essential to develop a 'body feel' for the action as soon as possible, and to be able to express it in your own words.

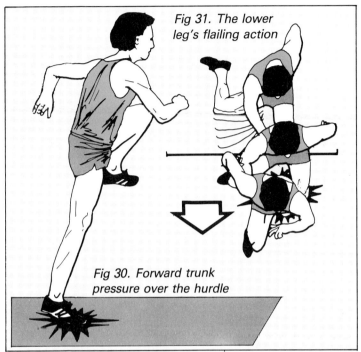

Fig 31. The lower leg's flailing action

Fig 30. Forward trunk pressure over the hurdle

A strong horizontal thrust at the hurdle is at the heart of the technique. It establishes the all-important flat flight-path (see figure 26). Figure 31 shows the flailing action of the lower leg — here the 'feel' words are:

- 'Drive' the heel at the hurdle!
- 'Karate-like' lower leg
- Get it up — get it down!

The hurdler must come off the hurdle running — flowing, high-hipped into the next barrier. The action between hurdles should be automatic — the more so the better.

Speed training for hurdles

It is difficult to separate speed-training for hurdling from the skill of hurdling itself. Speed-training schedules for hurdling correlate closely with those for sprinting. The essential difference probably lies in the volume of speed-endurance training which relates more to the longer sprints, for the 110 metres of the hurdle distance makes fewer demands than the 200-metre flat distance. Such training is best done over the hurdles rather than in pure sprinting.

These drills are specifically for hurdle-speed:

1 Starting Run in on the first hurdle, stressing hip height — 'run tall'.

2 Starting Run in on the first hurdle, stressing high leg-cadence — 'fast legs'.

3 Starting Bring the first hurdle in closer, so that you are forced to move your legs faster and to speed up your lead-leg action.

4 Leg-speed practice As an extension of drill 3, above, bring 3-6 hurdles in closer. These leg-speed practices are useful at the beginning of the training period (October to November) so that the rhythm of the event is preserved at a time when the hurdler is not fully fit. They are also of value at the other end of the training programme, when there is a need to sharpen leg-speed as competition time approaches.

5 Leg-speed practice Space the hurdles for five snappy strides between hurdles. The distance between hurdles here is arbitrary and can be adjusted according to your fitness level at any given time.

Speed, plyometrics and weights
These should be carried out as in the sprint schedules with particular stress on leg-speed practices.

Fig 32. The fast straight-line pick-up of the leading thigh

Hurdle-training tips

1 Drill the first eight strides to the hurdle until you make them automatic — they are the core of the race where you establish your rhythm.

2 Work with other hurdlers — this helps everyone in the group, quickening up the hurdling rhythms. Remember, however, to make only the final section of any training session 'competitive', otherwise, there is a danger of losing sight of your technical objectives.

3 Work on one particular point at a time. Do not be afraid, for instance, of spending a whole session working on the consistency of your start.

4 Use a 'blocking' technique (see Isolation Drills, page 36), as for sprints. This will help you to fovus in on the 'tunnel' which is your lane.

5 Unless you are working on starting technique, never train over less than three hurdles. Remember, this is a rhythm event!

6 Practise your finishes too — races can be won at the finish. This means making your 'dip' into the tape completely automatic.

400 metres hurdles

This distance is termed 'intermediate' in hurdles, and presents the athlete with a problem of a totally different nature from 110 metre hurdling. Unlike the sprint-hurdles, there are no obligatory stride-patterns — balance and control are at the core of success in this event.

If we check the stride-patterns of the 1968-1976 Olympic finalists, the nature of the problem emerges. In 1968, David Hemery, in the thin air of Mexico City, produced a world record of 48.1 seconds using 13 strides to the eighth hurdle, moving up to 15 strides for the final five. This 'change down' meant 'losing' about 4 metres. Part of this distance was lost by natural fatigue, but most of it (at least between hurdles 5-8) had to be lost by a marginal shortening on each stride. These adjustments were almost impossible to detect, so skilfully did Hemery make them. Had he made them clumsily, perhaps involving a running-on-the-spot action or a series of long and then short strides, he would have lost speed. Equally important, Hemery would have arrived at each barrier in the wrong position for an efficient clearance — with subsequent loss of speed.

So, speed in 400 metre hurdles is not simply a matter of tacking 400-metre flat speed on to an efficient hurdling technique. It depends on finding a stride pattern which lets you express that technique, and on good spatial judgement.

In the 1972 Munich Olympics, John Akii Bua (Uganda) decided that the 13-15 technique involved too much stride-adjustment and settled instead on a break-down to 14 strides at the fifth hurdle. This meant moving on to the 'weak' leg at the sixth barrier. Akii Bua stayed on this pattern — strong leg at the seventh — until the ninth hurdle (strong leg) when he reverted to a 15-stride pattern, bringing him on to his strong leg for the rest of the race. This stride pattern more accurately reflected Akii Bua's natural fatigue level, but required considerable hurdling skill of the weak leg.

By 1976, evolution had brought Ed Moses, the innovator of 13 strides between the barriers all the way. This was only possible because of Moses' massive natural stride-length. Indeed, the differential between Moses' 400-metre flat speed and his 400-metre hurdle time is probably now well below 2.0 seconds.

The times for the first 200 metres of Moses (23.0 seconds) and Hemery (23.1 seconds) are almost identical (see table 11). It is in the final four hurdles, where Moses' natural stride-

Table 11   Stride patterns

A comparison of monitored 400-metre hurdle stride patterns

	Moses		Akii Bua		Hemery	
Hurdle 1	6.0	20 strides	6.1	21 strides	6.0	21 strides
2	9.8	(3.8)	9.8	(3.7)	9.8	(3.8)
3	13.6	(3.8)	13.6	(3.8)	13.6	(3.8)
4	17.5	(3.9)	17.4	(3.8) 13 strides	17.5	(3.9) 13 strides
5	21.4	(3.9) 13 strides	21.3	(3.9)	21.5	(4.0)
(200m)	(23.1)		(23.0)		(23.3)	
6	25.5	(4.1) 13	25.4	(4.1)	25.4	(3.9)
7	29.6	(4.1)	29.5	(4.1) 14 strides	29.6	(4.2)
8	33.9	(4.3)	33.7	(4.2)	33.9	(4.3) 15 strides
9	38.2	(4.3)	38.1	(4.4) 15 strides	38.3	(4.4)
10	42.7	(4.5)	42.6	(4.5)	42.8	(4.5)
Run-in	(4.9)		(5.2)		(5.8)	
Time	47.64		47.82		48.1	
1st 200m	23.10		23.00		23.30	
2nd 200m	24.50		24.80		24.80	
Differential (2nd 200m- 1st 200m)	1.4		1.8		1.5	

length most ideally suits the distance between barriers, that the big difference shows. The run-in times (Moses 4.9 seconds and Hemery 5.8 seconds) also show that Moses holds speed much more effectively than Hemery.

There has to be a balance between the first and second halves of the race. This is illustrated by two British representatives in the women's 400-metre hurdles at the 1984 Los Angeles Olympics. After a poor finish, it emerged that Gladys Taylor and Sue Morley had differentials of close to 5 seconds! Table 11 shows a recommended series of 'splits' and first/second 200-metre distance differentials.

Finally, central to good intermediate hurdling is spatial awareness. Here the hurdler and the long-jumper have much in common. Neither sport is simply a matter of having an automatic pattern. Headwinds, back winds, or no wind at all, all mean that the hurdler must judge space. The more effectively he does this, the more fluent and relaxed he is, and ultimately, the more efficient his running and hurdling become. So the hurdler must 'see' the hurdle early and make the minor adjustments required to come into each hurdle in perfect balance.

CHAPTER TEN

Long jump

Long jump is a specialized development of a fast sprint — the essential feeling to have, though, is that of the fast sprint flowing out into a jump — not a sprint followed by a high jump. This will only reduce your speed as you go into the take-off — and this is fatal to the long-jumper.

High basic speed is vital — no world-class jumper is likely to run much slower than 10.60 seconds for 100 metres — but a successful long-jumper needs more. Bob Beamon, whose massive jump of 8 metres 90 centimetres set a long-standing world record at the Mexico Olympics, generally registered at least 0.6 seconds slower than Carl Lewis over 100 metres. This spectacular jump was the product of high take-off speed and massive lift — it was a one-off for a man who could not guarantee a jump of much more than 8 metres 20 centimetres. Carl Lewis, on the other hand, has regularly jumped beyond 8 metres 50 centimetres.

Robert Emmiyan, the Russian, who recorded the next longest jump of 8 metres 86 centimetres, however, has much less basic sprinting speed than Lewis, at 10.40 seconds for 100 metres. His take-off velocity is not as high, but he undoubtedly has greater lift at take-off.

The secret of success is speed both on and off the board — and to achieve this, you should look at all aspects of the approach run.

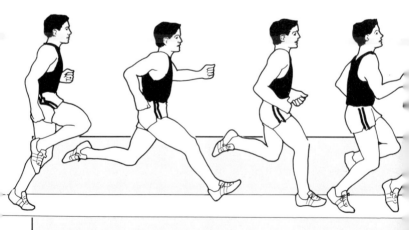

Table 12   Run-up strides related to speed

Speed over 100m	Number of strides
10.0-10.5 seconds	21-24
10.5-11.0 seconds	19-21
11.0-11.5 seconds	17-20
11.15-12.0 seconds	16-19
12.0 12.5 seconds	15-17
12.5-13.0 seconds	13-16

A correlation of springing speeds and the number of run-up strides taken.

Length of run

Depending on your speed over 100 metres, you will need to plan a run-up of more or less strides (see table 12) — as a rule, the faster you sprint, the more strides you should take.

You may well ask why this is, when top sprinters only reach top speed at 45-50 metres. It is because the long-jumper cannot use the extra speed — what he uses is a high, controllable fraction of his total speed.

The thing to aim for is getting on to the board at speed and in balance, so giving the best possible ability to compress the spring on take-off. This means the take-off foot hitting the maximum amount of board with the minimum braking and still keeping the trunk in a vertical position. At international level this means hitting the board at a speed of over 10 metres a second — this takes skill and judgement!

Fig 33. An early visual pick-up of the board allows a strong, balanced approach

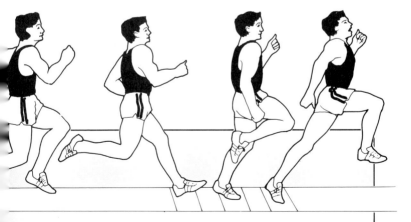

Spatial awareness

What are the factors involved in smacking a long jump board at speed? One of them is certainly the ability to judge space at high speed and make the fine adjustments to your run to make its crescendo perfect. Even at high level you can see competitors make late or misjudged decisions and consequently spoil their performance by fouling, losing speed, failing to reach the board or taking off in poor balance.

If the knack can be summarized in a feeling, it is that of 'locking in' with the eyes to judge a really powerful attack on the board. It's a form of awareness — not just looking, and is something you must develop in training.

You need to develop a feel for where the board is as early as possible in the run, so you can make gradual adjustments. The earlier you make these adjustments, the better you can 'lock in' for a really aggressive approach.

Jump structure

If you are a beginner, first plan your run and jump by running the appropriate number of strides back from the take-off point — have a friend count the steps with you. Run back and try to jump. The run-back will never be quite the same as the run-out, simply because of the adjustments you make for the take-off.

The simplest aim for the beginner is
RUN — HOLD SPEED — SPRING OUT.

By 'spring out' I mean that the take-off should be a drive out and away from the springing leg — not just an all-out attempt at height. The old rule of thumb used to be 'run fast, jump high', but the speed and height factors are mutually defeating to some extent — in trying to gain height, the

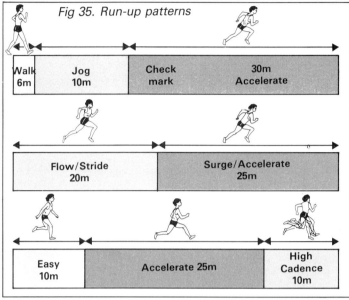

Fig 35. Run-up patterns

| Walk 6m | Jog 10m | Check mark | 30m Accelerate |

| Flow/Stride 20m | Surge/Accelerate 25m |

| Easy 10m | Accelerate 25m | High Cadence 10m |

jumper often tends to slow down. Far better is a flowing movement which literally 'springs out'.

You'll notice that world-class jumpers use a variety of starting positions, from the walk or jog-on to the stride start and the flat-out start — there's no absolute recipe for success which suits everyone.

Some jumpers walk or jog to a mark then seem to attempt to accelerate all the way on to the board. Others take a standing start, flow gradually into top speed, then increase their leg-cadence, attempting to hold speed into the board.

Fig 34. Sequence of long-jump balance and action

Another option is to adopt a fast stride for about eleven paces, then to accelerate into the board (see figure 35). The aim common to all of these is to achieve maximum possible speed at take-off, in dynamic balance.

This balance is vital — there's only one-tenth of a second available to apply all forces for take-off — and to do this effectively you need balance, which is directly related to the judgements made in the approach to the board.

Assuming you have made your approach judgements correctly, you arrive in balance and can stay tall as you reach the board. Inevitably your hips will drop as you near the board, but this should not be a conscious movement. The feeling to aim for is that of staying tall and fast all the way to the board.

As you take off, keep your body and head in line with the take-off drive. This way you get an efficient thrust of energy through the body's centre of gravity. If you kinked your spine or threw your head back, your take-off speed and balance would suffer.

The next feeling to achieve is that of a drive out and away from the board, but clinging to it for as long as possible behind the hips. Speed should still be there, working with the power of take-off to propel you out. Remember, the foundations of good long-jumping are approach-run and take-off — once you master these, you are 90% of the way there.

Training for long jump

General training for the long jump must relate closely to sprint training — working on speed and explosive power — but with consideration to other elements.

There's no obvious element of speed-endurance for the long-jump — the distances covered in the approach-runs of 30-50 metres seem to make no demands on this part of condition. Reaction-speed is of no importance. However, general endurance does play a part. When you train, the best development comes from making a good number of practice jumps in succession — you learn from each previous jump. It's therefore valuable to train, albeit in low volume, for general physical endurance.

Although it's useful to make a number of practice jumps using 50-60% of the full approach-run, jumps using 80-100% run-up, relate much more closely to competitive jumping — they have the speed and structure of a competition jump.

The alternative is to make 'dummy' runs without a jump, so that you can drill the basic structure of the approach.

CHAPTER ELEVEN

Triple jump

The triple jump has much in common with the long jump. The aim of long-jumpers and triple-jumpers are identical — to reach the board at maximum controlled speed. Everything about the structure of long jump approach-runs therefore applies directly to the triple jump — consequently training is the same.

The basic difference lies in the aim at take-off — the long-jumper is taking off at an angle of 20° and above, the triple-jumper at only 15-18°. Now, no triple-jumper has the slightest idea of whether he is jumping at 15° or 18°, any more than the long-jumper knows if he is jumping at 19-24°. What the triple-jumper does know is whether or not he is hopping too high or too low, since in the triple jump, hopping too high translates itself into a loss of distance in the step and jump.

Figure 36 shows a typical top-class triple jump, with a rough breakdown of 37% hop, 30% step and 33% jump. The aim in the hop is to gain maximum distance at the same time achieving minimum height. The 'feel' is of a drive-out or run-out from the board, which forms the essence of horizontal speed in the triple jump.

Balance

What the triple-jumper should also know is whether or not he is in balance when he strikes the board, and this relates largely to how well he has judged the space between himself and the board in the final 9-13 strides. The triple-jumper, like the long-jumper, must try to make subtle, almost imperceptible, changes in his strides in order to 'lock in' to his surge into take-off. The bigger those changes are, the more problems the jumper will have in finding the right take-off posture.

Triple-jumpers are possibly even more dependent than long-jumpers on finding a good take-off position, as they need to drive out of one phase into the next.

Bad board positioning often means a poor landing at the end of the hop. This, in turn, results in a struggle into the step followed by a weak, off-balance final jump. The jumper has to 'see' the board early, make his adjustments, then 'lock in' to a drive which takes him into and out of the take-off, and into his jump sequence.

Training for triple jump

The triple jump relates mostly to balanced sprinting speed, so sprint training is the main foundation. Certainly, reaction speed is of no importance in this event. However, although there is no obvious element of speed-endurance in the triple jump — the distance covered in approach-run (30-50 metres) make no demands on this element — it does have some place. This is because, in training, it is best to keep practice jumps close together to facilitate learning. The work programmes appropriate to speed-endurance are therefore of value, albeit in lower volumes.

Jump 1

Jump 2

Fig 36. Triple jump balance and action sequence

Jump 1

Jump 2

Jump 3

CHAPTER TWELVE

Weight-training

A solid base of weight-training can provide exactly the sort of explosive strength needed for good sprinting technique.

When you undertake weight-training, always go into the session with a routine of warm-up and stretch exercises, followed by some light-resistance, high-repetition work.

A weights session should run as follows:

a Warm-up and stretch
b Light-resistance, high-repetition work
c Central exercises (see weight exercises)
d Light-resistance work
e Jog and stretch

Weight exercises

The central exercises are as follows:

● Bench press (see figure 37)
● Squats (see figure 38)
● Power cleans (see figure 39/40)
● Strict curls (see figure 41)

Perform these in 3 or 4 sets each of 8-10 repetitions. Carry them out explosively, with good technique.

Note: Always wear a lifting-belt when performing weights exercises.

Bench press
Take the weight from stands or a partner to straight, wide arms, inhaling as you lower the weight on to a high chest. Then push up explosively, exhaling.

Fig 37. Bench press

Squats

Squat exercises are always potentially dangerous, so they are best done using a rack or squat-stands — otherwise you must have support from a partner. Lower to a position where your trunk and thighs form a right angle or above (never below), breathing in.
Drive up hard, breathing out.
Keep the back flat and the head up.

Fig 38. Squat exercise

Power cleans

Place the hands on the bar at just beyond shoulder-width. Keep your back flat, head up and feet flat on the ground. Make a drive up, fully straightening the legs, followed by a fast snap of the elbows and backs of the knees to 'catch' the weight. Breathe in on the effort and out on lowering the weight (this latter should also be done with the back flat, head up).

a   b   c   d   e

Fig 39/40. Figures a, b and c — High pull; Figures a, b, c, d and e — Power clean

Strict curls

Place the hands shoulder-width apart. Curl the bar up hard, pulling in the elbows, breathing out on the effort and in on the recovery. You must not allow any swing or leaning forward.

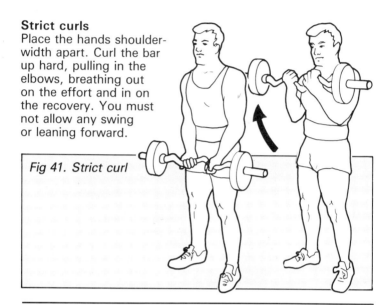

Fig 41. Strict curl

Stretches and high-repetition work

These exercises prepare you to do heavier-duty work without injury during the main session.

Sit-ups

Strong abdominals are essential to the sprinter! Use high repetition sets of abdominal exercises for warming up and for cooling down routines, after the main 'meat' of the programme of weights.

Dumb-bell punch

(see figure 42)
This is a light warm-up exercise. Carry out 3 sets of 10-15 repetitions, with 3-4 minutes between sets. Perform using a very light weight.

Fig 42. Dumb-bell punch

Fig 43. Back extension

Back extensions (see figure 43)
These are high-repetition exercises for warming up and
cooling down. You must achieve a full range of movement
and control in the recovery stage. Breathe in on the effort and
out on recovery.

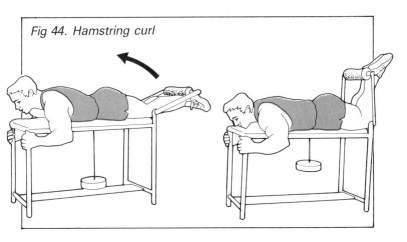

Fig 44. Hamstring curl

Hamstring curl (see figure 44)
This is an essential exercise which balances the development
of the extensor muscles of the front of the thigh. You do,
however, need to perform them on a machine in order to
carry them out effectively.

CHAPTER THIRTEEN

Circuit training

The main aim of circuit training is to provide a solid base of local and cardio-vascular fitness as a platform upon which to perform high-quality work in training and competition.

It is important to perform a variety of different types of circuit, not only to focus on different parts of the body, but to keep training fresh and exciting.

Remember, it is essential to use the correct technique in all circuits — the exercises serve you little purpose if you do not perform them properly.

General circuit

8-10 exercises — as many repetitions as possible of each exercise in 20 seconds, followed by 30 seconds rest. Take 5 minutes rest between circuits, building to 6 circuits.

Pyramid circuit

An advanced circuit with 10 repetitions of 3 exercises, with no

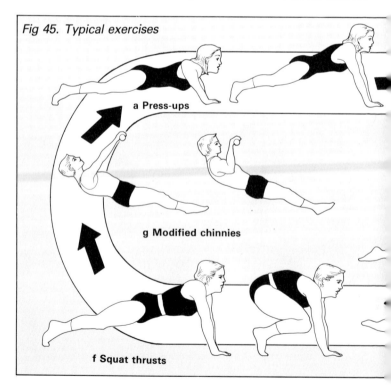

Fig 45. Typical exercises

a Press-ups

g Modified chinnies

f Squat thrusts

recovery between exercises, building up to 15-20 repetitions.

Plyometric circuit
These exercises require fast, explosive execution — clap press-ups, knee-tucks, hopping and bounding. The duration of each exercise is short — 15-20 seconds, with longish recovery times (30-45 seconds). As the season approaches, lengthen recovery times to 45-90 seconds.

Specific body-part conditioning
These relate to a specific part of the body — this might mean a circuit of say, 20-30 seconds per exercise, which pumps the arms — for example, strict-curls, high pulls or press-ups.

Stage training
Perform 5-10 repetitions of an exercise, with 30 seconds rest between each of the 3 sets, After 30 seconds rest, move on to the next 3 sets.

Varied repetition circuit
This circuit involves both maximums and timed efforts. Aim for 3 circuits, building to 5.

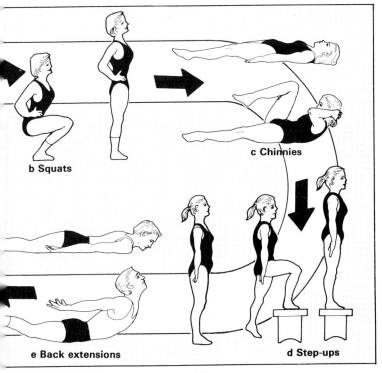

b Squats

c Chinnies

e Back extensions

d Step-ups

CHAPTER FOURTEEN

Plyometrics

Plyometrics have particular relevance to acceleration, although long bounding and hopping (50-100 metre distances) do have an effect on speed-endurance too.

Knee tucks (figure 46)
Best done on a resilient surface such as grass, mats or synthetic track. Drop to a quarter squat and immediately explode upwards, attempting to touch the palms of the hands. On touching the ground, treat it as if it were a red-hot stove and drive upwards. Perform 2-4 sets of 10-20 repetitions, taking 2 minutes rest between sets.

Fig 46. Knee tucks

Box bounds (figure 47)
This calls for four boxes, 40-70 centimetres high, placed 1-1.5 metres apart, and a soft landing surface. Jump up on the box and spring high from it, with full extension. On landing, recoil immediately and explosively, up on to the next box. Perform 4-6 sets, allowing 2 minutes rest between sets.

Fig 47. Box bounds

Multiple jumps (figure 48)
Jog in slowly, the trunk vertical, then make flat-footed
bounds, maintaining posture, stressing high knee-swing and a
feel of cling, cling, cling, with the grounded foot. Do this over
a distance of 20-50 metres, in 3-4 sets of 4-6. Allow 2 minutes
rest between sets.

Fig 48. Multiple jumps

Split jumps (figure 49)
Adopt a starting position, one leg extended, forward leg
flexed to 90°. Spring up and, on regaining position, spring up
again. Perform 2 or 3 sets of 5-8 jumps. Allow two minutes
rest between sets. An alternative is scissor-jumps, where
there is an alternate leg-split.

Fig 49. Split jumps

Dumb-bell arm swings (figure 50)
Dumb-bells of 5-10 lb weight are best for this exercise. Drive
the arms back and forwards, stopping at shoulder level on the
upswing. Make sure that you keep the arm bent on the
backswing. Keep the action rapid and rhythmic. Perform 2-4
sets of 20-30 swings, allowing 2 minutes between sets.

Fig 50. Dumb-bell swings

CHAPTER FIFTEEN

Mobility

Exercises for mobility are basically stretches. Their particular advantage for the sprinter is that they increase the range of movement in the limbs, they diminish the likelihood of injury and increase the muscles' capacity to relax.

There are three distinct types of mobility exercise:

1 Active   Here you actively press yourself into the end positions.

2 Passive   Here you use a partner, who presses you into the end positions.

3 Kinetic   For these exercises, you swing your limb into the necessary position at speed, using its own momentum.

In active and passive exercises you should hold the position for 20 seconds, followed by complete relaxation. Only attempt mobility exercises after a sustained jog of at least 5 minutes to warm up — and wear a track-suit and/or tights to help hold muscle heat and hence assist suppleness.

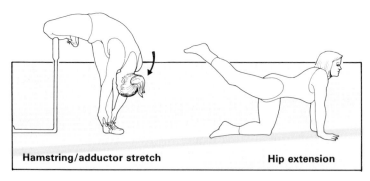

Hamstring/adductor stretch   Hip extension

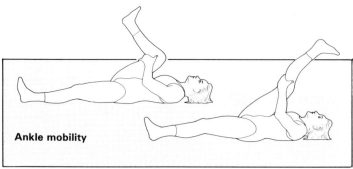

Ankle mobility

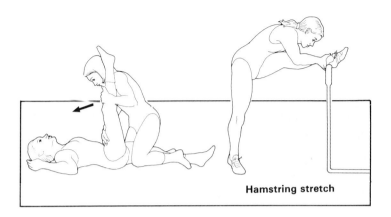

Hamstring stretch

Training tips

1 Remember that you cannot fire a cannon from a canoe! Your running needs a solid base of conditioning, involving weights, stretching, plyometrics, circuit-training and interval running to be the platform from which you develop speed later.

2 Quality is more important than quantity, particularly in the short sprints.

3 Keep a training diary, recording not only training details, but also your fatigue levels.

4 Balance your training schedules, making sure that heavy sessions are followed by light ones, or by sessions which work on another area of the body — for example, an arm and shoulder exercise period following a heavy running session.

5 Always warm up thoroughly — make it a ritual — and end each session with a jog and stretch. It can pay dividends in minimizing the risk of injury.

6 Make short and long-term aims for yourself. Enter each session with a clear purpose and have clear technical or conditioning aims for each session and work to them.

7 Remember that practice does not make perfect — practice makes permanent. So drill yourself in good habits and stop at any point in a session where your form is deteriorating.

8 After injury, do not be afraid to move back a few pages in your training. Remember too, that if one part of your body is injured, you should still work the other parts — weights, cycling, swimming can all help maintain condition during injury.

Index

A

Acceleration practices............20
Aerobic and anaerobic
   endurance.......................18
Anatomy of speed 8
Arm power........................21

C

Circuit training 74

F

Fat 15
Fatigue..............................14
Finish................................26
Four hundred metre hurdles....60
Four hundred metres............27
Four hundred metres break-
   down 28

H

Hurdle, first........................54
Hurdle technique 53
Hurdle training tips 59
Hurdles..............................52

I

Isolation drills......................36
   Arm impulse drill 39
   Blocking drill....................45
   Curve drill 45
   Driving practice drill 41
   Elbow drive drill................39
   Hand fix drill....................37
   Head and trunk drill 37
   High knee pick-up drill........42
   Jelly jaw drill 40
   Leg power........................21
   Leg speed drill 41
   Lift drill..........................42
   Lower leg drill..................43
   Potato crisp drill 38
   Reaction drill 44

L

Low jump 62
Long jump, training for..........66

M

Mental pictures 19
Middle-distance running........46
Middle-distance speed drills 50
Middle race technique 26
Mobility 21, 78
Muscle make-up.................. 8
Muscle power 11
Muscles and skeletal system ...12

P

Plyometrics 22, 76
Pure speed......................... 5

R

Race tactics, 400 metres 29
Relay competition.................34
Relay training schedules........35

S

Speed, charisma of.............. 6
Speed drills 48
Speed, feel of...................... 7
Speed training for hurdles 57
Speed training for women 6
Sprint speed........................18
Sprinting............................18
Start 23
Starting speed 19
Starting technique and
   position.........................24
Stretching exercises 72

T

Training intensity 7
Triple jump..........................67

W

Warm up 16
Weight training 70